Aids to the Stud

Maya Codices

Cyrus Thomas

Alpha Editions

This edition published in 2024

ISBN : 9789366386768

Design and Setting By
Alpha Editions
www.alphaedis.com
Email - info@alphaedis.com

INTRODUCTION.

The object of this paper is to present to students of American paleography a brief explanation of some discoveries, made in regard to certain Maya codices, which are not mentioned in my previous papers relating to these aboriginal manuscripts.

It is apparent to every one who has carefully studied these manuscripts that any attempt to decipher them on the supposition that they contain true alphabetic characters must end in failure. Although enough has been ascertained to render it more than probable that some of the characters are phonetic symbols, yet repeated trials have shown beyond any reasonable doubt that Landa's alphabet furnishes little or no aid in deciphering them, as it is evidently based on a misconception of the Maya graphic system. If the manuscripts are ever deciphered it must be by long and laborious comparisons and happy guesses, thus gaining point by point and proceeding slowly and cautiously step by step. Accepting this as true, it will be admitted that every real discovery in regard to the general signification or tenor of any of these codices, or of any of their symbols, characters, or figures, or even in reference to their proper order or relation to one another, will be one step gained toward the final interpretation. It is with this idea in view that the following pages have been written and are now presented to the students of American paleography.

It is impracticable to present fac simile copies of all the plates and figures referred to, but it is taken for granted that those sufficiently interested in this study to examine this paper have access to the published fac similes of these aboriginal documents.

CHAPTER I.

THE NUMERALS IN THE DRESDEN CODEX.

Before entering upon the discussion of the topic indicated it may be well to give a brief notice of the history and character of this aboriginal manuscript, quoting from Dr. Förstemann's introduction to the photolithographic copy of the codex,261-1 he having had an opportunity to study the original for a number of years in the Royal Public Library of Dresden, of which he is chief librarian:

"Unfortunately, the history of the manuscript begins no further back than 1739. The man to whom we owe the discovery and perhaps the preservation of the codex was Johann Christian Götze, son of an evangelical pastor, born at Hohburg, near Wurzen, in the electorate of Saxony. He became a Catholic, and received his education first at Vienna, then in Rome; became first chaplain of the King of Poland and elector of Saxony; later on, papal prothonotary; presided over the Royal Library at Dresden from 1734, and died holding this position, greatly esteemed for learning and integrity, July 5, 1749. This sketch is taken from his obituary notice in Neue Zeitungen von gelehrten Sachen, Nr. 62, Leipzig, 1749. In his capacity as librarian he went to Italy four times, and brought thence rich collections of books and manuscripts for the Dresden library. One of these journeys took place in 1739, and concerning its literary results we have accurate information from a manuscript, in Götze's handwriting, which is found in the archives of the Royal Public Library, under A, Vol. II, No. 10, and bears the title: 'Books consigned to me for the Royal Library in January, 1740.' Under No. 300 we read: 'An invaluable Mexican book with hieroglyphic figures.' This is the same codex which we here reproduce.

"Götze also was the first to bring the existence of the manuscript to public notice. In 1744 he published at Dresden The Curiosities of the Royal Library at Dresden, First Collection. As showing what value Götze attributed to this manuscript, the very first page of the first volume of this work, which is of great merit and still highly useful, begins as follows: '1. A Mexican book with unknown characters and hieroglyphic figures, written on both sides and painted in all sorts of colors, in long octavo, laid orderly in folds of 39 leaves, which, when spread out lengthwise, make more than 6 yards.'

"Götze continues speaking of this book from page 1 to 5, adding, however, little of moment, but expatiating on Mexican painting and hieroglyphic writing in general. On page 4 he says:

"'Our royal library has this superiority over all others, that it possesses this rare treasure. It was obtained a few years ago at Vienna from a private person, for nothing, as being an unknown thing. It is doubtless from the personal effects of a Spaniard, who had either been in Mexico himself or whose ancestors had been there.'

"On page 5 Götze says:

"'In the Vatican library there are some leaves of similar Mexican writing, as stated by Mr. Joseph Simonius Asseman, who saw our copy four years ago at Rome.'

"Götze therefore received the manuscript as a present on his journey to Italy at Vienna and took it with him to Rome. Unfortunately we know nothing concerning its former possessor. A more accurate report of the journey does not seem to exist; at least the principal state archives at Dresden contain nothing concerning it, nor does the General Directory of the Royal Collections. As appears from the above note, Götze did not know that the Vatican Codex was of an entirely different nature from the Dresden Codex.

"In spite of the high value which Götze set upon the manuscript, it remained unnoticed and unmentioned far into our century. Even Johann Christoph Adelung, who as head librarian had it in his custody and who died in 1806, does not mention it in his Mithridates, of which that part which treats of American languages (III, 3) was published only in 1816, after Adelung's death, by J. S. Vater. This would have been a fitting occasion to mention the Dresden Codex, because in this volume (pp. 13 et seq.) the Maya language is largely treated of, and further on the other languages of Anahuac. Of course it was not possible at that time to know that our manuscript belongs to the former.

"After Götze, the first to mention our codex is C. A. Böttiger, in his Ideas on Archæology (Dresden, 1811, pp. 20, 21), without, however, saying anything that we did not already know from Götze. Still Böttiger rendered great and twofold service: first, as we shall see presently, because through him Alexander von Humboldt obtained some notice of the manuscript, and, second, because Böttiger's note, as he himself explains in the Dresden Anzeiger, No. 133, p. 5, 1832, induced Lord Kingsborough to have the manuscript copied in Dresden.

"We now come to A. von Humboldt. His Views of the Cordilleras and the Monuments of the Indigenous Peoples of America bears on the title page the year 1810, which certainly means only the year in which the printing was begun, the preface being dated 1813. To this work, which gave a mighty impulse to the study of Central American languages and literatures, belongs the Atlas pittoresque, and in this are found, on page 45, the reproductions of five pages of our manuscript. They are Nos. 47, 48, 50, 51, and 52 of Lord Kingsborough. In the volume of text belonging to this atlas Humboldt discusses our manuscript on pp. 266, 267. When he began his work he knew nothing as yet of the existence of the manuscript. It was brought to his knowledge by Böttiger, whose above named work he cites. Here we learn for the first time that the material of the manuscript consists of the plant metl (*Agave Mexicana,*) like other manuscripts that Humboldt had brought from New Spain. Furthermore, he correctly states the length of leaf as 0.295 and the breadth 0.085 meter. On the other hand, he commits two mistakes in saying that there are 40 leaves and that the whole folded table forming the codex has a length of almost 6 meters, for there are only 39 leaves and the length in question is only 3.5 meters, as calculation will approximately show, because the leaves are written on both sides. Humboldt's other remarks do not immediately concern our problem.

"In 1822 Fr. Ad. Ebert, then secretary and later head librarian, published his History and Description of the Royal Public Library at Dresden. Here we find, as well in the history (p. 66) as in the description (p. 161), some data concerning this 'treasure of highest value,' which indeed contain nothing new, but which certainly contributed to spread the knowledge of the subject among wider circles. We may remark right here that H. L. Fleischer, in his Catalogue of Oriental Manuscript Codices in the Royal Library of Dresden, p. 75, Leipzig, 1831, 4°, makes but brief mention of our codex, as 'a Mexican book of wood, illustrated with pictures, which awaits its Œdipus;' whereupon he cites the writing of Böttiger. The signature of the manuscript here noted, E 451, is the one still in use.

"Between the above mentioned notices by Ebert and Fleischer falls the first and so far the only complete reproduction of the manuscript. Probably in 1826, there appeared at Dresden the Italian Augustino Aglio, a master of the art of making fac similes by means of tracing through transparent substances. He visited the European libraries, very probably even at that time under orders from Lord Kingsborough, to copy scattered manuscripts and pictures from Mexico or seemingly from Mexico.

"Now there arises the question, all important for interpretation, In which shape did the manuscript lie before Aglio? Was it a strip only 3.5 meters in length or did it consist of several pieces?

"To render clear the answer which we proceed to give, it is first necessary to remark that of the 39 leaves of the codex 35 are written on both sides and 4 on one side only, so that we can speak only of 74 pages of manuscript, not of 78. These 74 pages we shall in the following always designate by the numbers which they bear in Lord Kingsborough, and it is advisable to abide by these numbers, for the sake of avoiding all error, until the manuscript can be read with perfect certainty; the 4 empty pages I shall designate with 0 when there is need of mentioning them expressly.

"Furthermore it is necessary to state which of these pages so numbered belong together in such way that they are the front and back of the same leaf. This condition is as follows: One leaf is formed of pages 1 45, 2 44, 3 43, 4 42, 5 41, 6 40, 7 39, 8 38, 9 37, 10 36, 11 35, 12 34, 13 33, 14 32, 15 31, 16 30, 17 29, 18 0, 19 0, 20 0, 21 28, 22 27, 23 26, 24 25, 46 74, 47 73, 48 72, 49 71, 50 70, 51 69, 52 68, 53 67, 54 66, 55 65, 56 64, 57 63, 58 62, 59 61, 60 0. [That is to say, each pair of this series forms one leaf, one page on one side and the other on the reverse side of the leaf.]

"But now we are justified in the assumption, which at least is very probable, that neither did Aglio change arbitrarily the order of the original, nor Lord Kingsborough the order of Aglio. Consequently Aglio must already have had the manuscript before him in two pieces, be it that the thin pellicles by which the single leaves are connected were loosened in one place or that the whole was separated only then in order not to be obliged to manipulate the whole unwieldy strip in the operation of copying. A third possibility, to which we shall presently return, is that of assuming two separate pieces from the beginning; in this case Götze and the others must be supposed to have seen it in this condition, but to have omitted the mention of the circumstance, believing that the original unity had been destroyed by tearing.

"Of the two pieces one must have comprised 24, the other 15 leaves. But Aglio copied each of the two pieces in such way as to trace first the whole of one side and then the other of the entire piece, always progressing from left to right, in European style. Therefore Aglio's model was as follows:

"*First piece*:

"Front (from left to right): 1, 2, 3, 4, 5, 6, 7, 8, 9, 10, 11, 12, 13, 14, 15, 16, 17, 18, 19, 20, 21, 22, 23, 24.

"Back (from right to left): 45, 44, 43, 42, 41, 40, 39, 38, 37, 36, 35, 34, 33, 32, 31, 30, 0, 0, 0, 28, 27, 26, 25.

"*Second piece*:

"Front (from left to right): 46, 47, 48, 49, 50, 51, 52, 53, 54, 55, 56, 57, 58, 59, 60.

"Back (from right to left): 74, 73, 72, 71, 70, 69, 68, 67, 66, 65, 64, 63, 62, 61, 0.

"In considering this, our attention is attracted by the position of the four blank pages, three of which are together, the fourth alone. It might be expected that the separate blank page began or concluded the second piece and was purposely left blank, because in the folding of the whole it would have lain outside and thus been exposed to injury; the other three would be expected at the end of the first piece. The former, as is easily seen, was quite possible, but the latter was not, unless we assume that even at the time Aglio took his copy the original order had been entirely disturbed by cutting and stitching together again. The four blank pages show no trace of ever having contained writing; the red brown spots which appear on them are to be found also on the sides that contain writing. Perhaps, therefore, those three continuous pages indicate a section in the representation; perhaps it was intended to fill them later on; in a similar way also page three has been left unfinished, because the lower half was only *begun* by the writer.

"I do not wish to conceal my view that the two pieces which Aglio found were separated from the beginning; that they belong even to two different manuscripts, though written in the same form; but, since it is human to err, I will here and there follow custom in the succeeding pages in speaking of one codex.

"My conviction rests especially on the fact that the writer of manuscript A (pp. 1-45) endeavors to divide each page by two horizontal lines into three parts, which the writer of manuscript B (pp. 46-74) rarely does. The more precise statement is as follows: In A, pp. 1-23 and 29-43 always show two such lines in red color; pp. 25-28 have no red lines, but clearly show a division into three parts; p. 24 is the only one of this manuscript that has only writing and no pictures and where the greater continuity of the written speech forbids tripartition (here ends one side of the manuscript); finally, p. 45 seems to be marked as the real end of the whole by the fact that it contains three very light lines, dividing it into four parts; moreover, everything on this page is more crowded, and the figures are smaller than on the preceding pages, just as in some modern books the last page is printed more closely or in smaller type for want of space. In the same manner I suspect that p. 1 is the real beginning of the manuscript. This is indicated by the bad condition of leaf 2 44, which has lost one corner and whose page 44 has lost its writing altogether. For, if in folding the codex leaf 1 45 was turned from within outward, somewhat against the rule, leaf 2 44 was the outer one, and p. 44 lay above or below, and was thus most exposed to injury. I will not omit mentioning that my attention has been called by Dr. Carl Schultz-Sellack, of Berlin, to the possibility of leaves 1 45 and 2 44 having been fastened to the rest in a reversed position, so that 43, 1 and 2 and on the other side 44, 45, 3 were adjoining; then the gods would here be grouped together, which follow each other also on pages 29 and 30. It cannot be denied that this supposition explains the bad condition of leaf 2 44 still better, because then it must have been the outermost of the manuscript; 44 would be the real title page, so to say, and on p. 45 the writer began, not ended, his representation, with the closer writing of which I have spoken, and only afterward passed on to a more splendid style; and this assumption tallies very well with some other facts. But all this can only be cleared up after further progress has been made in deciphering the manuscript.

"In two places, moreover, this first manuscript shows an extension of the drawings from one page over to the neighboring one, namely, from 4 to 5 and from 30 to 31. This is not found on the second manuscript. From continuity of contents, if we are allowed to assume it from similarity of pictures and partition, we may suppose this manuscript to be divided into chapters in the following manner: pp. 1-2 (then follows the unfinished and disconnected page 3), 4-17, 18-23 (here follows p. 24, without pictures), 25-28, 29-33, 34-35, 36-41.

"Compared with this, manuscript B rarely shows a tripartition, but on pp. 65-68 and 51-57 a bipartition by one line. A further difference is this, that A out of 45 pages has only one (p. 24) without pictures, while B out of 29 pages has 9 without pictures (51, 52, 59, 63, 64, 70, 71, 72, 73), nothing but writing being found on them. Page 74, differing from all others, forms the closing tableau of the whole; and, similarly, p. 60, the last of the front, shows a peculiar character. A closer connection of contents may be suspected between pp. 46-50, 53-58, 61-62, 65-68.

"The two manuscripts also differ greatly in the employment of the sign, or rather signs, differing little from each other, which resemble a representation of the human eye and consist of two curves, one opening above and the other below and joined at their right and left ends. These signs occur only on 5 out of the 45 pages of Codex A (1, 2, 24, 31, 43), while they occur on 16 pages out of the 29 of Codex B (48, 51, 52, 53, 55, 57, 58, 59, 61, 62, 63, 64, 70, 71, 72, 73).

"I believe that the differences above mentioned, to which others will probably be added, are sufficient to justify my hypothesis of the original independence of the two codices. Whoever looks over the whole series of leaves without preconception cannot escape the feeling, on passing from leaf 45 to leaf 46, that something different begins here.

"Thus the copy of Aglio has made it possible to venture a hypothesis bordering on certainty concerning the original form of this monument. Five years after Aglio had finished the copying there appeared, in 1831, the first volumes of Lord Kingsborough's Mexican Antiquities. The work in the trade cost 175*l.*; the expense of publication had been over 30,000*l.* The eighth and ninth volumes followed only in 1848. The ponderous work has undoubtedly great value from its many illustrations of old monuments of Central American art and literature, which in great part had never been published. As regards the Spanish and English text, it is of much less value. We may pass in silence over the notes added by Lord Kingsborough himself, in which he tries to give support to his favorite hypothesis that the Jews were the first settlers of America. Whoever wishes to obtain exact information concerning the character and contents of the whole work and dreads the labor of lifting and opening the volumes, may find a comprehensive review of it in the Foreign Quarterly Review, No. 17, pp. 90-124, 8vo, London, January, 1832, where he will also find a lucid exposition of the history of the literature of Mexican antiquarian studies.

"In the middle of the third volume of the Mexican Antiquities (side numbers are here absent) there is found the title 'Fac simile of an original Mexican painting preserved in the Royal Library at Dresden, 74 pages.' These 74 pages are here arranged on 27 leaves in the following manner:

Codex A.	Codex B.
1, 2, 3,	46, 47, 48,
4, 5, 6,	49, 50, 51,
7, 8, 9,	52, 53, 54,
10, 11,	55, 56, 57,
12, 13, 14,	58, 59, 60,
15, 16, 17,	61, 62, 63,
18, 19,	64, 65, 66,
20,	67, 68, 69,
21, 22, 23,	70, 71, 72,
24, 25,	73, 74.
26, 27, 28,	
29, 30, 31,	
32, 33, 34,	
35, 36, 37,	
38, 39, 40,	
41, 42, 43,	
44, 45.	

"On the whole, therefore, each leaf in Kingsborough comprises three pages of our manuscript. Why the publisher joined only two pages in the case of 10 and 11, 18 and 19, 24 and 25, and left page 20 entirely separate, I cannot say; but when he failed to add 46 to 44 and 45 it was due to the fact that here there is indication of a different manuscript.

"On January 27, 1832, Lord Kingsborough wrote a letter from Mitchellstown, near Cork, in Ireland, to Fr. Ad. Ebert, then head librarian at Dresden, thanking him again for the permission to have the manuscript copied and telling him that he had ordered his publisher in London to send to the Royal Public Library at Dresden one of the ten copies of the work in folio. The original of the letter is in Ebert's manuscript correspondence in the Dresden library.

"On April 27, 1832, when the copy had not yet arrived at Dresden, an anonymous writer, in No. 101 of the Leipziger Zeitung, gave a notice of this donation, being unfortunate enough to confound Humboldt's copy with that of Lord Kingsborough, not having seen the work himself. Ebert, in the Dresden Anzeiger, May 5, made an angry rejoinder to this "hasty and obtrusive notice." Böttiger, whom we mentioned above and who till then was a close friend of Ebert, on May 12, in the last named journal, defended the anonymous writer (who perhaps was himself) in an extremely violent tone. Ebert's replies in the same journal became more and more ferocious, till Böttiger, in an article of May 25 (No. 150 of the same journal), broke off the dispute at this point. Thus the great bibliographer and the great archæologist were made enemies for a long time by means of our codex.

"From Kingsborough's work various specimens of the manuscript passed into other books; thus we find some in Silvestre, Paléographie universelle, Paris, 1839-'41, fol.; in Rosny, Les écritures figuratives et hiéroglyphiques des peuples anciens et modernes, Paris, 1860, 4to; and also in Madier de Montjou, Archives de la société américaine de France, 2de série, tome I, table V.

"In 1834 Ebert died, and was followed as head librarian by K. C. Falkenstein. He, unlike his predecessor, strove especially to make the library as much as possible accessible to the public. Visits and examinations of the library became much more frequent, and our manuscript, being very liable to injury, on account of its material, had to be withdrawn from the hands of visitors, if it was desired to make it accessible to their sight. It was therefore laid between glass plates and thus hung up freely, so that both sides were visible. In this position it still hangs in the hall of the library, protected from rude hands, it is true, but at the same time exposed to another enemy, daylight, against which it has been protected only in recent time by green screens. Still it does not seem to have suffered much from light during these four decades; at least two former officers of the library, who were appointed one in 1828 and the other in 1834, affirm that at that time the colors were not notably fresher than now. This remark is important, because the coloring in Humboldt, as well as in Lord Kingsborough, by its freshness gives a wrong impression of the coloring of the original, which in fact is but feeble; it may have resembled these copies some 300 years ago.

"In 1836, when the manuscript was being preserved in the manner indicated, the two unequal parts, which were considered as a whole and which no one seems to have thought susceptible of being deciphered, were divided into two approximately equal parts from considerations of space and for esthetic reasons.

"The first five leaves of Codex A, that is, pp. 1-5, with the backs containing pp. 41-45, were cut off and prefixed to Codex B in such way as to have p. 46 and p. 5 adjoining; when I examined the codex more closely I found that between 5 and 46, and therefore also between 41 and 74, there was no such pellicle as generally connects the other leaves. By this change one part was made to contain 20 leaves, the other 19.

"At the same time another change was made. The three blank pages between pp. 28 and 29 had a marring effect, and they were put at the end by cutting through between leaves 18 0 and 17 29 and turning the severed leaves around, so that p. 24 joined on to p. 29 and 17 to 25. The pellicle loosened on this occasion was fastened again.

"I must expressly state that I have no written or oral account of these two manipulations, but conclude they have taken place merely from a comparison of the present arrangement with that which Aglio must have had before him.

"Thus the arrangement in which I found the manuscript, which it may be best to preserve until my views are recognized, is the following:

"(1) *The diminished Codex A (19 leaves)*:

Front: 6, 7, 8, 9, 10, 11, 12, 13, 14, 15, 16, 17, 25, 26, 27, 28, 0, 0, 0.

Back: 18, 19, 20, 21, 22, 23, 24, 29, 30, 31, 32, 33, 34, 35, 36, 37, 38, 39, 40.

"Or, if we enumerate the numbers on the back from right to left, so that the back of each leaf stands beneath its front:

6,	7,	8,	9,	10,	11,	12,	13,	14,	15,	16,	17	25,	26,	27,	28,	0,	0,	0.
40,	39,	38,	37,	36,	35,	34,	33,	32,	31,	30,	29	24,	23,	22,	21,	20,	19,	18.

"(2) *The enlarged Codex B (20 leaves)*:

Front: 1, 2, 3, 4, 5, 46, 47, 48, 49, 50, 51, 52, 53, 54, 55, 56, 57, 58, 59, 60.

Back: 0, 61, 62, 63, 64, 65, 66, 67, 68, 69, 70, 71, 72, 73, 74, 41, 43, 43, 44, 45.

"Or, reversing, as in the preceding case, the numbers on the back:

1,	2,	3,	4,	5	46, 47, 48, 49, 50, 51, 52, 53, 54, 55, 56, 57, 58, 59, 60.
45,	44,	43,	42,	41	74, 73, 72, 71, 70, 69, 68, 67, 66, 65, 64, 63, 62, 61, 0."

One of the most difficult things to account for in regard to this codex is the immense number of numeral characters it contains, many of which appear to have no reference to day or other time symbols.

Although it is not claimed that the key which will fully unlock this mystery has been found, it is believed that the discoveries made will throw considerable light on this difficult subject and limit the field of investigation relating to the signification of the Maya codices.

Before proceeding with the discussion of the subject proposed, it will not be amiss to state, for the benefit of those readers not familiar with these ancient American manuscripts, that the Maya method of designating numbers was by means of dots and lines, thus: • (one dot) signifying one; • • (two dots) two, and so on up to four; five was indicated by a single short straight line, thus, ▬; ten, by two similar lines, ▭; and fifteen, by three such lines: ▤ . According to this system, a straight line and a dot, thus, ▬•, would denote 6; two straight lines and two dots, ▤, 12; and three straight lines and four dots, ▤, 19. But these symbols do not appear to have been used for any greater number than nineteen. They are found of two colors in all the Maya codices, one class black, the other red, though the latter (except in a few instances, where the reason for the variation from the rule is not apparent) are never used to denote a greater number than thirteen, and refer chiefly to the numbers of the days of the Maya week and the numbers of the years of the "Indication" or "week of years." On the other hand, the black numerals appear to be used in all other cases where numbers not exceeding nineteen are introduced. As will appear in the course of this discussion, there are satisfactory reasons for believing that other symbols, quite different from these dots and lines, are used for certain other numbers, at least for 20 and for 0.

In order that the reader may understand what follows, it is necessary to explain the methods of counting the days, months, and years in the order in which they succeed one another. Much relating to this will be found in a previous work,[269-1] but a particular point needs further explanation.

According to the older and also the more recent authorities, the Maya years—there being 20 names for days and 365 days in a year—commenced alternately on the first, sixth, eleventh, and sixteenth of the series, that is to say, on the days Kan, Muluc, Ix, and Cauac, following one another in the order here given; hence they are spoken of as Kan years, Muluc years, Ix years, and Cauac years.

Writing out in the form of an ordinary counting house calendar the 365 days of the year, commencing with 1 Kan and numbering them according to the Maya custom (that is, up to thirteen to form their week and then commencing again with one) they would be as shown in Table I.

TABLE I.—*Names and numbers of the months and days of the Maya system.*

	Pop.	Uo.	Zip.	Tzoz.	Tzec.	Xul.	Yaxkin.	Mol.	Chen.	Yax.	Zac.	Ceh.	Mac.	Kankin.	Muan.	Pax.	Kayeb.	Cumhu.	Numbers of days
	1	2	3	4	5	6	7	8	9	10	11	12	13	14	15	16	17	18	
Names of the days.																			
Kan	1	8	2	9	3	10	4	11	5	12	6	13	7	1	8	2	9	3	1
Chicchan	2	9	3	10	4	11	5	12	6	13	7	1	8	2	9	3	10	4	2
Cimi	3	10	4	11	5	12	6	13	7	1	8	2	9	3	10	4	11	5	3
Manik	4	11	5	12	6	13	7	1	8	2	9	3	10	4	11	5	12	6	4
Lamat	5	12	6	13	7	1	8	2	9	3	10	4	11	5	12	6	13	7	5
Muluc	6	13	7	1	8	2	9	3	10	4	11	5	12	6	13	7	1	8	6
Oc	7	1	8	2	9	3	10	4	11	5	12	6	13	7	1	8	2	9	7
Chuen	8	2	9	3	10	4	11	5	12	6	13	7	1	8	2	9	3	10	8
Eb	9	3	10	4	11	5	12	6	13	7	1	8	2	9	3	10	4	11	9
Been	10	4	11	5	12	6	13	7	1	8	2	9	3	10	4	11	5	12	10
Ix	11	5	12	6	13	7	1	8	2	9	3	10	4	11	5	12	6	13	11
Men	12	6	13	7	1	8	2	9	3	10	4	11	5	12	6	13	7	1	12
Cib	13	7	1	8	2	9	3	10	4	11	5	12	6	13	7	1	8	2	13
Caban	1	8	2	9	3	10	4	11	5	12	6	13	7	1	8	2	9	3	14
Ezanab	2	9	3	10	4	11	5	12	6	13	7	1	8	2	9	3	10	4	15
Cauac	3	10	4	11	5	12	6	13	7	1	8	2	9	3	10	4	11	5	16
Ahau	4	11	5	12	6	13	7	1	8	2	9	3	10	4	11	5	12	6	17
Ymix	5	12	6	13	7	1	8	2	9	3	10	4	11	5	12	6	13	7	18
Ik	6	13	7	1	8	2	9	3	10	4	11	5	12	6	13	7	1	8	19
Akbal	7	1	8	2	9	3	10	4	11	5	12	6	13	7	1	8	2	9	20
Intercalated days.																			
Kan																	10		
Chicchan																	11		
Cimi																	12		
Manik																	13		
Lamat																	1		

Each of these eighteen columns forms one month, and the whole taken together, with the 5 days added at the end of the eighteenth month, form one continuous series, the second column following the first as though placed at the end of it, the third following the second, and so on to the end of the eighteenth. Whether or not it was the ancient custom to include the 5 added days in the year, as asserted by the old Spanish writers, is somewhat doubtful, at least in studying the Dresden Codex, we shall find but few occasions, if any, to use them, for there are few if any positive indications in this codex that they were added.

As stated, each column of the table forms a month, though the numbering is carried to thirteen only; but at present the chief object in view in presenting it is to use it in explaining the method of counting the days and the intervals of time. The table is in truth a continuous series, and it is to be understood as though the 365 days were written in one column, thus:

1.	Kan.
2.	Chicchan.
3.	Cimi.
4.	Manik.
5.	Lamat.
6.	Muluc.
7.	Oc.
8.	Chuen.
9.	Eb.
10.	Been.
11.	Ix.
12.	Men.
13.	Cib
1.	Caban.
2.	Ezanab, &c.,

the 20 days being repeated over and over in the order in which they stand in the table. This order is never changed; we may commence at whatever point in the series occasion may require, but the order here given must always be maintained, just as in our calendar the order of our days is always Sunday, Monday, Tuesday, &c. In other words, Chicchan must always follow Kan, Cimi must always follow Chicchan, &c.

The method of counting intervals in the Maya calendar is very simple, if these explanations are borne in mind, and may be illustrated thus: Counting 14 days from 1 Kan—the first day of the year given in Table I—brings us to 2 Ezanab (the day we count from being excluded); 12 days more bring us to 1 Oc, in the second column of our table; 17 days more to 5 Manik, in the third column; and 17 days more, to 9 Kan, in the fourth column.

The number of the day required is readily ascertained by adding together the number of the day counted from and the number of days to be counted, casting out the thirteens when the sum exceeds this number (excepting where the remainder is thirteen); thus: $1 + 14 - 13 = 2$, the number of the day Ezanab given above. So $1 + 14 + 12 - 13 - 13 = 1$, the number of the day Oc, second column, Table I; and $1 + 14 + 12 + 17 + 17 - 13 - 13 - 13 - 13 = 9$, the number of the day Kan, fourth column. The reason for this is so apparent that it is unnecessary to state it.

Suppose the day counted from is 11 Muluc of the eleventh month, and the number of days to be counted (or the interval) is 19; by adding together the numbers and casting out the thirteens the following result is obtained: $11 + 19 - 13 - 13 = 4$. Counting forward on the table 19 days from 11 Muluc (the sixth number in the eleventh figure column), we reach 4 Lamat (the fourth day of the twelfth month). When the sum of the numbers is a multiple of 13 the number obtained is 13, as there can be no blanks, that is to say, no day without a number.

As the plates of the codices are usually divided into two or three compartments by transverse lines, it is necessary to adopt some method of referring to these in order to avoid the constant repetition of "upper," "middle," and "lower" division. On the plan proposed by Dr. Förstemann, in his late work on the Dresden Codex (Erläuterungen zur Mayahandschrift der Königlichen öffentlichen Bibliothek zu Dresden), these divisions are designated by the letters *a*, *b*, and *c*; this plan will be adopted in this paper. The letter *a* joined to the number of a plate, therefore, will signify that the division referred to is the upper one, as Plate 12*a*; the letter *b* signifies the middle one where there are three divisions or the lower one where there are but two; and the letter *c* signifies the lowest or bottom division where there are three.

Where reference is made to the fac simile of the Dresden Codex, Kingsborough's colored edition is always to be understood, except where another is specially mentioned.

Running through Plates 36*c* and 37*c* is a continuous line of day symbols and red and black numeral characters as follows, the numbers and names below the characters being explanatory and of course not on the original:

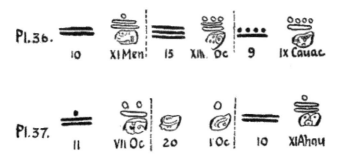

FIG. 359. Lines of day and numeral symbols.

As colors are not used in these figures the red numerals are indi cated by hollow or outline dots and lines and the black numerals by solid lines and dots.272-1

In order further to assist those unacquainted with the symbols the same line is here given in another form, in which the names of the days are substituted for the symbols, Roman numerals for the red numbers, and Arabic for the black: 10, XI Men; 15, XIII Oc; 9, IX Cauac; 11, VII Oc; S, I Oc; 10, XI Ahau.

The S is introduced to represent a numeral symbol different from the lines and dots and will be explained when reached in the course of the illustration.

Starting from 11 Men, found in the twelfth figure column of Table I, and counting forward fifteen days, we come to 13 Oc of the thirteenth figure column, the second day of the above quoted line. Counting nine days from 13 Oc273-1 brings us to 9 Cauac, the third day of the line; eleven days more, to 7 Oc, the fourth day of the line. Following this day in the line, instead of a black numeral of the usual form, is this symbol: ![symbol] represented by S in the second form, where the names and numbers are substituted for the symbols. Taking for granted, from the position it occupies in the line, that it is a numeral character, it must represent 20, as the day which follows is 1 Oc, and counting twenty days from 7 Oc brings us to 1 Oc. Counting ten days more we reach 11 Ahau, the last day of the line given above.

In this example the black numerals appear to have been used simply as counters, or as numbers indicating intervals; for example, 15 is the interval between 11 Men and 13 Oc.273-2

This furnishes a clew which, if followed up, may lead to important results. That it explains the signification of one symbol undetermined until this relation of the numerals to one another was discovered, is now admitted. In the work of Dr. Förstemann before alluded to the discovery of the symbol for 20 is announced. Although I was not aware of the signification of this symbol until after my second paper, "Notes on certain Maya and Mexican manuscripts," was written, I had made this discovery as early as 1884.273-3

As there will be occasion to refer to the days of the four different series of years (the Cauac, Kan, Muluc, and Ix years), a combined calendar, similar to an ordinary counting house calendar, is introduced here. For the Cauac years the left or Cauac column is to be used; for the Kan years, the Kan column, and so on.

TABLE II.—*Names and numbers of the four series of years of the Maya system.*

Cauac column.	Kan column.	Muluc column.	Ix column.	1 14	2 15	3 16	4 17	5 18	6	7	8	9	10	11	12	13	Numbers of the months.
																	Days of month.
Cauac	Kan	Muluc	Ix	1 8	2 9	3 10	4 11	5 12	6 13	7							1
Ahau	Chicchan	Oc	Men	2 9	3 10	4 11	5 12	6 13	7 1	8							2
Ymix	Cimi	Chuen	Cib	3 10	4 11	5 12	6 13	7 1	8 2	9							3
Ik	Manik	Eb	Caban	4 11	5 12	6 13	7 1	8 2	9 3	10							4
Akbal	Lamat	Been	Ezanab	5 12	6 13	7 1	8 2	9 3	10 4	11							5
Kan	Muluc	Ix	Cauac	6 13	7 1	8 2	9 3	10 4	11 5	12							6
Chicchan	Oc	Men	Ahau	7 1	8 2	9 3	10 4	11 5	12 6	13							7
Cimi	Chuen	Cib	Ymix	8 2	9 3	10 4	11 5	12 6	13 7	1							8
Manik	Eb	Caban	Ik	9 3	10 4	11 5	12 6	13 7	1 8	2							9
Lamat	Been	Ezanab	Akbal	10 4	11 5	12 6	13 7	1 8	2 9	3							10
Muluc	Ix	Cauac	Kan	11 5	12 6	13 7	1 8	2 9	3 10	4							11
Oc	Men	Ahau	Chicchan	12 6	13 7	1 8	2 9	3 10	4 11	5							12
Chuen	Cib	Ymix	Cimi	13 7	1 8	2 9	3 10	4 11	5 12	6							13
Eb	Caban	Ik	Manik	1 8	2 9	3 10	4 11	5 12	6 13	7							14
Been	Ezanab	Akbal	Lamat	2 9	3 10	4 11	5 12	6 13	7 1	8							15
Ix	Cauac	Kan	Muluc	3 10	4 11	5 12	6 13	7 1	8 2	9							16
Men	Ahau	Chicchan	Oc	4 11	5 12	6 13	7 1	8 2	9 3	10							17
Cib	Ymix	Cimi	Chuen	5 12	6 13	7 1	8 2	9 3	10 4	11							18
Caban	Ik	Manik	Eb	6 13	7 1	8 2	9 3	10 4	11 5	12							19
Ezanab	Akbal	Lamat	Been	7 1	8 2	9 3	10 4	11 5	12 6	13							20

As this table has been explained in my previous papers it is only necessary to add here that the thirteen figure columns form a single series; therefore, when we reach the bottom of the thirteenth column we go back to the top of the first. The day reached will be the one directly opposite (that is, in the same horizontal line) in the day column for the given year.

For example, taking the fifth column of numbers (the one having 3 for the top figure) and counting down nine days from the top number we reach the number 12. This will be 12 Lamat if a Cauac year, 12 Been if a Kan year, 12 Ezanab if a Muluc year, and 12 Akbal if an Ix year. Therefore it is necessary in counting to refer always to the year (year column) with which the count begins. So long as the particular year referred to is unknown (as is Usually the case, the day series being apparently of general rather than of special application) it is immaterial which day column is selected, as the result will be the same with any. This will be apparent if we bear in mind that, when 260 days with their numbers attached have been written down in proper order as a series, we have therein all the possible combinations of days and numbers. This, it is true, does not give us all the months and years (to include these it is necessary to write out fifty-two entire years), but the same series of numerals will be applicable to each of the four year series (Kan, Muluc, Ix, and Cauac years). As any one of the thirteen figure columns of the table may be taken as the commencement of a year and any of the four day columns may be used, it is apparent that we have all the possible combinations (4 × 13 = 52).

I say above that "it is necessary in counting to refer always to the year (year column) which the count begins." This I admit does not agree with the generally received idea of the Maya calendar, upon which Table II is constructed, as, according to this theory (which I have accepted in my previous papers), after passing through a year of one series (corresponding with one of the day columns of the table), we should enter upon a year of the next series; for example, when the year 1 Kan is completed we should enter upon the year 2 Muluc.

Although this calendar system seems to have been in vogue at the time of the conquest and is indicated in one or two of the codices, and possibly in the one now under consideration, the chronological series of the latter, as will hereafter appear, do not seem to be based upon it or to agree with it.

These explanations, with the further statement that the lines in the codex are to be read from left to right and the columns from the top downward, except where variations from this rule are noted, will enable the reader to follow the discussion. Another reason for using a table with only thirteen columns (though it would be difficult to devise a combined calendar of any other form) is that the 260 days they contain form one complete cycle, which, as will appear in the course of this discussion, was one of the chief periods in Maya time computations.

Examining Plates 33 to 39 of the codex the reader will observe that the line already alluded to extends continuously through division *c*, commencing with the two characters over the figure (picture) in the lower right hand corner of Plate 33.

The first of these characters as given in Kingsborough's work is the symbol of the day Ezanab, with the red numeral 13 to the left of it and the black numeral 9 over it; but referring to Förstemann's photolithographic copy of the codex it is found to be the symbol of Ahau.

The entire line, with this correction (that is to say, as given by Förstemann), is represented in Fig. 360. In order to assist the reader, the names of the days and numbers of the symbols have been added immediately below the characters.

As the year to which the line relates is unknown, we select the Muluc series, designated "Muluc column" in Table II, and commence with 13 Ahau, the twelfth number of the third figure column. Counting 9 days from this brings us to 9 Muluc, the top number of the fourth figure column and also the second day of the line above given. (the symbol is a face in Kingsborough's copy, but is plainly the Muluc sign in Förstemann's photograph). Eleven days more bring us to 7 Ahau, the third day of the above line; 20 more to 1 Ahau, the fourth day of the line (the 20 here is the symbol represented by S); 10 more to 11 Oc, the fifth day of the line; 15 more to 13 Chicchan, the sixth day of the line; 9 more to 9 Ix, the seventh day of the line; 11 more to 7 Chicchan, the eighth day of the line; line; 20 (S) more to 1 Chicchan, the ninth day of the line; 10 more to 11 Men, the tenth day of the line, and so on to the end.

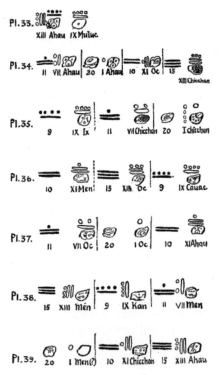

FIG. 360. Line of day and numeral characters.

- 18 -

That the order of the series may be clearly seen the numbers are given here as they stand in the line, omitting the days: XIII; 9, IX; 11, VII; 20, I; 10, XI; 15, XIII; 9, IX; 11, VII; 20, I; 10, XI; 15, XIII; 9, IX; 11, VII; 20, I; 10, XI; 15, XIII; 9, IX; 11, VII; 20, I; 10, XI; 15, XIII.

By adding together a black numeral and the preceding red one and casting out thirteen (or thirteens, as the case maybe), when the sum exceeds this number, we obtain the following red one, thus: XIII + 9 - 13 = IX; IX + 11 - 13 = VII; VII + 20 - 13 - 13 = I; I + 10 = XI, and so on through the entire series. Attention is also called to the fact that the sum of the black (Arabic) numbers 9, 11, 20, 10, 15, 9, 11, 20, 10, 15, 9, 11, 20, 10, 15, 9, 11, 20, 10, 15, is 260, a multiple of 13.

If this relation of days and numerals holds good as a general thing throughout the codex, it is apparent that where the break is not too extensive it will enable the student to restore the missing and defective numerals and day symbols, to detect the errors of both copyists and original artists, and to determine the proper relation of the plates to one another. By it he learns, as before stated, that the symbol (see page 273) denotes 20, and if phonetic probably stands for the Maya word *Kal*.

Comparing Plates 42 and 43 with Plates 1 and 2, the resemblance is found to be so strong as to lead to the belief that they belong together. It is apparent from the figures, numerals, and characters277-1 in the middle division (*b*) of Plates 1 and 2 that they belong together, as they now stand in Kingsborough's work and Förstemann's copy; that Plates 42 and 43 are properly placed in regard to each other is also apparent from the figures and numerals in divisions *a* and *b*.

Taking for granted that the lines are to be read from left to right and the plates to follow each other in the same order, our next step is to ascertain on which side of the pair (Plates 42 and 43) Plates 1 and 2 should be placed.

The series of days and of numbers in Plate 43*b* and Plate 1*b*, which evidently belong together, can only be brought into proper relation by placing the latter to the right of the former. Yet, strange as it may appear, the days and numerals in this division are to be read from right to left, while all the other numeral series of these four plates are to be read as usual, from left to right. This change in the order of the pages also brings together the similar figures in the upper division of these plates. That Plate 42 properly follows Plate 41 is apparent from the line of alternate red and black numerals in division *b*. As shown in a previous work278-1 and as will appear hereafter, these horizontal lines of alternate red and black numerals without day symbols interspersed are usually, if not always, connected at the left with a column of days over which there is a red numeral, as in the Codex Troano. Running back along the line of numerals in the middle division of Plates 42 and 41, the day column with which it is connected is found at the left margin of Plate 38. Unfortunately the red numeral over this column is obliterated, but can easily be restored. Starting with the first black numeral to the right of this, the entire line, which ends in the second column of the middle division of Plate 43 (representing the black numerals by Arabic numbers and the red by Roman numbers), is as follows: 16, IX; 8, IV; 11, II; 10, XII; 1, XIII; 12, XII; 6, VI(?); 12, IV; 11, II; 11, XIII; 6, VI; 12, V; 7, XII; 6, V; S + 1, XIII; 6, VI.

The number over the day column, Plate 38, must have been VI, as VI + 16 - 13 = 9, a conclusion which is sustained by Förstemann's copy, which shows here very plainly the red character for VI.

By adding the black (Arabic) numeral to the preceding red (Roman) one and casting out the thirteens, as heretofore explained, we obtain the following red (Roman) numerals, thus: VI + 16 - 13 = IX; IX + 8 - 13 = IV; IV + 11 - 13 = II; II + 10 = XII; XII + 1 = XIII; XIII + 12 - 13 = XII; XII + 6 - 13 = V.

Here the result differs from what is found at this point in the line, as we obtain V instead of VI. In this case the mistake, if one has been made, cannot be attributed to Lord Kingsborough's copyist; the Maya artist must have made a mistake or there must be an error in the theory here advanced. But let us continue according to our own figures: V + 12 - 13 = IV; IV + 11 - 13 = II; II + 11 = XIII; XIII + 6 - 13 = VI; VI + 12 - 13 = V; V + 7 = 12; XII + 6 - 13 = V; V + 20 + 1 - 13 = XIII; XIII + 6 - 13 = VI.

There is no doubt, therefore, that the line forms one continuous series, and if so it links together pages 38 and 43 as they are now numbered. It follows, then, that if Plates 1 and 2 and Plates 42 and 43 belong together, the former pair must be placed to the right of 43. This is conceded by Dr. Förstemann,278-2 as he says that, Dr. Karl Schultz-Sellack having pointed out the error in his paging, he changed pages 1 and 2 to 44 and 45 and pages 44 and 45 to 1 and 2; that is to say, the two leaves containing these pages were loosened from the strip and reversed, so that page 1 would be 44 and page 2 would be 45.

Having brought together these plates so that 1 and 2 stand to the right of 43, attention is called to the lines of day symbols running through division c. Substituting names and numbers as heretofore, they are as follows:

Plate 42:	IV Ahau;	XII Lamat;	VII Cib;	II Kan;	X Eb;	V Ahau;	XIII Lamat.
	17	8	8	8	8	8	8
Plate 43:	IV Chicchan;	XII Been;	VII Ymix;	II Muluc;	X Caban;	V Chicchan;	XIII Been.
	17	8	8	8	8	8	8

Plate 1:	IV Oc;	XII Ezanab;	VII Cimi;	II Ix;	X Ik;	V Oc;	(?) Ezanab.
	17	8	8	8	8	8	8
Plate 2:	IV Men;	XIII Akbal;	VII Chuen;	II Cauac;	X Manik;	V Men;	XIII Akbal.
	17	8	8	8	8	8	8

The chief objects in view at present in selecting this series are, as before indicated, to prove the relation of the plates to one another and to determine the use of the black numerals which stand under the day symbols. These numerals consist of but two different numbers, the first on each page being 17, the rest 8's.

As the particular year or years to which the series refers is unknown we turn to our calendar—Table II—and select the Kan column, as we find that 4 Ahau, the first day of the series, is the seventeenth day of the year 1 Kan. This corresponds with the first black numeral. Counting 8 days from this we reach 12 Lamat, the second day of our series; 8 more bring us to 7 Cib, the third day of the series; 8 more to 2 Kan; 8 more to 10 Eb; 8 more to 5 Ahau; 8 more to 13 Lamat, and 17 more to 4 Chicchan. The red numeral at this point in some of the colored copies of Kingsborough's work is III, but a close inspection shows the missing dot which has not been colored. IV Chicchan is therefore correct.

Continuing our count, 8 days more bring us to 12 Been: 8 more to 7 Ymix; 8 more to 2 Muluc; 8 more to 10 Caban; 8 more to 5 Chicchan; 8 more to 13 Been; 17 more to 4 Oc; 8 more to 12 Ezanab; 8 more to 7 Cimi; 8 more to 2 Ix; 8 more to 10 Ik; 8 more to 5 Oc, and 8 more to 13 Ezanab. Here the red numeral is wanting, but a comparison of the numbers on the different plates and the order of the series make it evident that it should be XIII.

Continuing our count, 17 more bring us to 4 Men (here a dot is missing in Kingsborough's copy, but is present in the photograph); 8 more to 12 Akbal. Here there is one dot too many, which we may attribute to a mistake of the original artist. Assuming XII to be correct, 8 more bring us to 7 Chuen; 8 more to 2 Cauac; 8 more to 10 Manik; 8 more to 5 Men; 8 more to 13 Akbal, and to the end of our table; thus, if we include the first seventeen days, completing the series of thirteen months or 260 days.

These illustrations will probably satisfy any one that the black numerals in these lines denote the intervals between the days indicated by the symbols and that the series so far examined are to be read from left to right.

Although the succession of days and numbers in the lines of the last example would seem to furnish conclusive evidence that the whole is one continuous series, yet the peculiar combinations of numbers used by the Maya priests render these series very deceptive. There can be no doubt that the black numbers—8's—are used to indicate the intervals between the days specified; but there is another possible way of explaining the 17 with which the lines on the different plates begin.

Here are four plates, evidently closely related to one another; the lines of days and numbers in the lowest division of each are precisely alike, except as to the days indicated; in the left hand column of characters of each is one of the cardinal point symbols. It is possible, therefore, that these four plates relate to the four different years or series of years; that is to say, one to the Kan years, one to the Muluc years, and so on. This view is somewhat strengthened by the fact that 4 Ahau, first of the line on Plate 42, is the seventeenth day of the first month of the year 1 Kan; 4 Chicchan, first of the line on plate 43, the seventeenth day of the first month of the year 1 Muluc; 4 Oc, the seventeenth day of 1 Ix, and 4 Men the seventeenth day of 1 Cauac. The four figures in the middle division of Plates 1 and 2 seem also to favor this idea, not so much by the peculiar animals represented (of which we have no explanation to give) as by the double symbols from which they are suspended, which I am quite confident denote the union of years or the time at which two years meet—the close of one and the commencement of another—although fully aware that Dr. Förstemann has interpreted them as symbols of the heavenly bodies.280-1

In the text above these figures are seen two characters or symbols of this type, which in all probability, as will hereafter appear, denote or symbolize the "tying of the years." We may also add that the five days of each plate or group are the five assigned, as I have explained in "Notes on certain Maya and Mexican manuscripts," to the cardinal points. For example, those on Plate 42 are Ahau, Eb, Kan, Cib, Lamat.280-2 Still it must be admitted, on the other hand, that as the four lines form precisely one complete cycle of 13 months or 260 days there is a very strong inference that they together form one continuous series and that the arrangement into four parts or divisions has reference to the four seasons or four cardinal points. The final decision on this point therefore still remains in doubt.

As it has been shown that Plates 33 to 39 and Plates 38 to 43 are properly placed as they stand in Kingsborough's copy and also in Förstemann's and that Plates 1 and 2 follow Plate 43, we have proof that the following plates succeed one another to the right, as here given: 33, 34, 35, 36, 37, 38, 39, 40, 41, 42, 43, 1, 2.

A slight inspection is sufficient to show that Plates 29 to 33 follow one another in the same order, a conclusion which is easily verified by testing the lines of numerals in the manner explained. It is apparent, therefore, that the following plates form one unbroken series, running from left to right: 29, 30, 31, 32, 33, 34, 35, 36, 37, 38, 39, 40, 41, 42, 43, 1, 2; a conclusion which Dr.

Förstemann, who has had the opportunity of studying the original, has now reached.

Having ascertained the object and use of at least one class of black numerals and the relation they bear to the days and day numbers, it may be well to test further the discovery by other examples, in order to see how far it holds good and what new facts it may bring out. In doing this it will be necessary to repeat in part what has already been shown by Dr. Förstemann in his late work; but as these discoveries were made independently and before this work came to hand, and as our conclusions differ in some respects from those reached by him, the plan and scope of this paper would be incomplete without these illustrations.

Commencing with the day column in the middle of Plate 35*b* and extending through Plates 36*b* and 37*b* to the right margin of the latter, is a line of alternate red and black numerals, which may be taken as an example of the most common series found in the Dresden and other codices. It is selected because it is short, complete, and has no doubtful symbols or numerals in it.

Using names and numbers in place of the symbols, it is as follows:

I.	
Caban,	11, XII; 6, V; 9, I; 4, V; 7, XII; 9, VIII; 6, I.
Muluc.	
Ymix.	
Been.	
Chicchan.	

In this case the red numeral over the day column is I. It is to be observed that the last number of the series is also I, a fact which it will be well to keep in mind, as it has an important bearing on what is now to be presented. But it is proper to show first that this series is continuous and is connected with the day column.

Adding the I over the column to the 11, the first black numeral; gives XII, the red numeral following the 11. That this holds good in all cases of this kind will become apparent from the examples which will be given in the course of this discussion. Adding together the remaining pairs, as follows: XII + 6 - 13 = V; V + 9 - 13 = 1; 1 + 4 = V; V + 7 = XII; XII + 9 - 13 = VIII; VIII + 6 - 13 = I, we obtain proof that the line is one unbroken series. It is apparent that if the black numerals are simply counters used to indicate intervals, as has been suggested, then, by adding them and the red numerals over the column together and casting out the thirteens, we should obtain the last red number of the series. In this case the sum of the numbers 1, 11, 6, 9,

4, 7, 9, 6, is 53; casting out the thirteens the remainder is 1, the last of the series. If we take the sum of the black numbers, which in this case is 52, and count the number of days on our calendar (Table II) from 1 Caban, the fourteenth day of the first month of the year 1 Kan, we shall find that it brings us to 1 Muluc, the sixth day of the fourth month; 52 days more to 1 Ymix; 52 more to 1 Been, and 52 more to 1 Chicchan, thus completing the day column in the example given. This proves, in this case at least, that the red numeral over the day column applies to all the days of the column and that the whole numeral series—that is to say, the sum of the counters— represents the interval between the successive days of the column. The total number of days from 1 Caban, first of the column, to 1 Chicchan, the last, is 208. Adding 52 more gives 260 and brings us back to 1 Caban, our starting point.

It will be observed that the sum of the black numbers—which denotes the interval between the days of the column—is 52, which is a multiple of 13, the number of days in a Maya week. It follows, therefore, that so far as this rule holds good the last red numeral of the series must be the same as that over the day column. In a former work282-1 I explained the method of ascertaining the relations of the days of a column to one another by means of the intervals without reference to the numbers attached to them, a subject to which Charency had previously called attention;282-2 by the explanation now given we ascertain the true intervals between the days *as numbered*. The two modes therefore form checks to each other and will aid very materially in restoring obliterated and doubtful days.

There is another point in regard to these series which may as well be illustrated by means of the example given as any other. What is the signification of the red numerals of the series? They are unnecessary if the only object in view was to indicate the intervals between the days of the column. Nor will the supposition that the Mayas had not discovered a means of representing higher numbers than 20 suffice, as the introduction of 13 would have lessened the labor and shortened the calculation. But one answer to this inquiry appears possible, viz, that these numbers are intended to denote certain intermediate days to which importance was for some reason attached. These intermediate days can readily be determined from the data given, and in the present example are as follows:

(1) Between 1 Caban and 1 Muluc they are 12 Lamat, 5 Ix, 1 Akbal, 5 Manik, 12 Ix, and 8 Akbal.

(2) Between 1 Muluc and 1 Ymix they are 12 Ahau, 5 Cimi, 1 Men, 5 Cauac, 12 Cimi, and 8 Men.

(3) Between 1 Ymix and 1 Been they are 12 Eb, 5 Ezanab, 1 Manik, 5 Chuen, 12 Ezanab, and 8 Manik.

(4) Between 1 Been and 1 Chicchan they are 12 Kan, 5 Oc, 1 Cauac, 5 Akbal, 12 Oc, and 8 Cauac.

These, as will be readily perceived, are found by counting on the calendar from 1 Caban, 1 Muluc, &c., as heretofore explained.283-1

Our interpretation of the series of this particular class is now complete, except as to their application or the object in view in forming them and the determination of the particular years to which they apply. Possibly they may be of general application, so far as consistent with the calendar system. The conclusion on this point depends largely upon the conclusion as regards the system, as it is evident their location in time—if the year of 365 days and the four series of years formed the basis of the system—would not correspond with their position in a system based upon the year of 360 days, in which the four year series does not play any necessary part.

Dr. Förstemann calls attention to the fact that the pairs of numerals representing the intermediate days are usually placed in separate compartments, each containing a figure or a picture generally symbolic or of a priest dressed to indicate some particular god. It is therefore very probable that these intermediate days are to be devoted to ceremonies relating to the divinities or subjects indicated by these figures.

In order to confirm the theory we are now discussing and at the same time show some of the different varieties of the series of the type now under consideration, the following additional examples are given.

In the middle division of Plate 5 is a day column and a numeral series, as follows:

I.		
Manik	}	
Cauac		16, IV; 9, XIII; S + 5, XII; 2, I.
Chuen		
Akbal		
Men		

This series terminates with I, as it should according to the theory. The sum of the black numerals—16, 9, 20, 5, 2—is 52, a multiple of thirteen, and the interval between the successive days, reading downwards, is 52, agreeing in these particulars with the theory. It will also be observed that the symbol represented by S answers to the number 20.

In the lowest division of the same plate is another similar series, as follows:

XII		
Ezanab	}	
Akbal		20 + 9, II; 11, XIII; 18, V; 7, XII.
Lamat		
Been		
Ezanab		

This terminates with XII, the number over the column; the sum of the black numbers is 65, a multiple of thirteen and precisely the interval between the successive days of the column, taking the week numbers into consideration, which is always to be understood in speaking of these intervals unless the contrary is expressly stated.

 FIG. 361.

In the middle division of Plate 8 is a short series connected with a day column containing the following days, reading downwards, as usual: Manik, Cauac, Chuen, Akbal, Men. The symbol for Akbal (Fig. 361), is a very unusual one, reminding us strongly of a skull, which may possibly have given origin to the symbol. The numerals of the series are as follows: 20 + 6, VIII; 20 + 6, VIII; the number over the column, VIII; and the interval between the days, 52.

In Plate 15, division c, is the following series, which differs from those given in having two day columns instead of one:

III	III		
Lamat	Ix		
Ahau	Cimi	}	12, II; 14, III.
Eb	Ezanab		
Kan	Oc		
Cib	Ik		

The final number is the same as that over the columns; the sum of the black numbers is 26, which is a multiple of 13; but in this case in counting the intervals the days are to be taken alternately from the two columns.

Commencing with 3 Lamat on our calendar and counting 26 days brings us to 3 Ix; 26 more to 3 Ahau; 26 more to 3 Cimi, and so on to the end.

In the lower division of Plate 9 is a series arranged as follows:

III	III		VI	VIII
Cauac	Been		3	2
Chuen	Chicchan	{	XI 3	II 4
Akbal	Caban	{	VI 4	VII 1
Men	Muluc		I	III
Manik	Ymix		7	2

The sum of the black numerals is 26 and the final red number is III, the same as that over the columns. The interval between the days, taken alternately from the two columns, as in the preceding example, is 26. The numbers are also to be taken alternately from the two number columns.

It is apparent that these examples sustain the theory advanced. This will also be found true in regard to all the series of this type in this and the other codices where the copy is correct. Brasseur's copy of the Manuscript Troano is so full of mistakes that no satisfactory examination of this codex can be made until a photographic copy is obtained; nevertheless a few examples are given as proof of the above statement.

In the third division of Plate XI* is the following series:

IV		
Ahau	}	
Eb		17, VIII; 13, VIII; 10 V; 12, IV.
Kan		
Cib		
Lamat		

As will be readily seen, after the explanations given, this agrees with the theory advanced.

The last red number is the same as that over the day column, the sum of the black numbers is 52, and the interval between the days 52.

Commencing in the right margin of the lowest division of Plate XXIII* and running through Plates XXII* and XXI*, is the series here represented:

VII	VII		
Cib	Cimi	}	
Ik	Eb		7, I; 7, VIII; 7, II; 5, VII.
Lamat	Ezanab		
Ix	Kan		
Ahau	Oc		

An examination of this shows it to be of the type of the double column series of the other codex, except that here the days of one column are to be taken in the order in which they stand before proceeding to the other column. The sum of the black numbers is 26 and the interval between 7 Cib and 7 Ik 26 days. The interval between 7 Ik and 7 Lamat, 7 Lamat and 7 Ix, and between 7 Ix and 7 Ahau is, in each case, 26 days. The interval between 7 Ahau, last day of the left hand column, and 7 Cimi, the first day of the right hand column, is also 26 days.

The order in which the days of these double column series of this manuscript follow one another is not uniform, as in some cases (see Plate XXV*, division *a*) they are to be taken alternately from the two columns, as in the examples heretofore given from the Dresden Codex.

In the middle division (Plate XXXIII*, same codex) is a series of the following form, but with the days so nearly obliterated that restoration is necessary:

			VI	I
			5	8
I			VI	I
Ymix (?)			5	8
Cimi (?)			VI	I
Chuen			5	8
Cib (?)			VI	I
(?)			5	8
			VI	I
			5	8

The symbol of the first day has only the upper circle of dots to indicate that it is Ymix, that of the second day is almost obliterated, the third is clearly

Chuen, the lower half of the fourth is obliterated, and the interior of the fifth is a blank.

Fortunately there are sufficient data by which to make the restoration. Chuen, we observe, is the middle of the column; that is, two days are above it and two days below it; the sum of the black numerals is 65; hence the interval between the days, considering the week numbers as attached, is 65, and the simple interval in the month series, without regard to the week numbers, is 5. Counting back on our calendar (Table II) 65 days from 1 Chuen we reach 1 Cimi, and 65 more bring us to 1 Ymix. In like manner we find the fourth day to be 1 Cib and the fifth 1 Ymix. The numbers in the figure columns are to be taken alternately, thus: 5, VI; 8, I; 5, VI; 8, I, &c.

These examples are sufficient to show that the series of the Manuscript Troano are arranged upon the same plan and based upon the same system as those of the Dresden Codex. The following examples from the Codex Cortesianus prove the same thing to be true in reference to the series found in it.

The first is taken from the lower division of Plates 10 and 11, Rosny's reproduction:

XIII		
Ahau Chicchan	}	11, XI; 5, III; 5, VIII; 5, XIII; 9, IX; 3, XII; 6, V; 1, VI; X, XIII.
Oc		
Men		

The S in the line of numerals represents the usual symbol for 20. The sum of the black numbers is 65, the interval between the days 65, and the last red numeral the same as that over the day column, thus agreeing in plan with those in the other codices.

The following double column series is found in the middle division of Plate 30:

XI	XI		
Ahau	Ymix	}	
Eb	Been		20 + 6, XI; 20 + 6, XI.
Kan	Caban		
Cib	Chicchan		
Lamat	Manik		

The number 20 is denoted by the usual symbol. The sum of the black numbers is 52 and the interval between the days in each column 52, but in this case there does not appear to be any connection between the columns, there being, in fact, two distinct series.

In the upper division of the same plate is this series:

XI			
Ezanab	{	VI 8	XI 5
Oc	{	VI 8	XI 5
Ik	{	VI 8	XI 5
Ix	{	VI 8	XI 5
Cimi			

The order in which these numerals are to be read is as follows: 8, VI; 5, XI; 8, VI; 5, XI, &c., which gives, as the final red number of the series, XI, the same as that over the column. The sum of the black numbers is 52 and the interval between the days 52.

Taking for granted that the correctness of the theory advanced is conceded, some attempts at its further application, especially its use in making restorations and corrections in defective series and in settling doubtful questions relating thereto, will now be presented.

In the upper division of Plate 32, Dresden Codex, are the four day columns and lines of numerals over them here represented:

1			
4	13	9	4
15	13	2	11
XIII	XIII	XIII	XIII
Manik	Cib	Chicchan	Ix
Chuen	Ahau	Muluc	Ezanab
Men	Kan	Been	Ik
Cauac	Lamat	Caban	Cimi
Akbal	Eb	Ymix	Oc

Connected with these numbers is a line of alternate black and red numbers running along over the figures of Plates 32 to 39, division *a*. There are several breaks and some partially obliterated characters in it which must be restored in order to use it. It has been selected partly on this account, that the method of filling such breaks and making such restorations may be seen.

Representing the numerals and symbols as heretofore and substituting a cipher where the numbers are wanting or are too much obliterated to be determined by inspection, the series will be as follows: 11, XI; 8 + 20, 0; 12 (or 13), XIII; 6 + 20, XIII; 12, VII (?); 16 (?), V; 5, X; 1, XI; 20, V; 12, IV, 6, X; 0, V; 5, X; 7, IV; 12 (?), II; 5, VII; 8, II; 11, 0.

Commencing with the XIII over the day columns and counting as heretofore, we obtain the following result: XIII + 11 - 13 = XI; XI + 8 + 20 - 13 - 13 = XIII. The first blank should therefore be filled with XIII. Continuing, XIII + 13 - 13 = XIII; the black numeral in this case should be 13, although apparently 12 in the codex; XIII + 6 + 20 - 13 - 13 = XIII; XIII + 12 - 13 = XII. Here the result obtained differs from the red numeral in the codex, which is apparently one line and two dots, or VII; but, by carefully examining it or inspecting an uncolored copy, the two lines which have been covered in the colored copy by a single broad red line are readily detected. The next black numeral is partially obliterated, the remaining portion indicating 16, but it is apparent from the following red numeral that it should be 19. Making this correction we proceed with our count: XII + 19 - 13 - 13 = V; V + 5 = X; X + I = XI; XI + 20 - 13 - 13 = V; V + 12 - 13 = IV; IV + 6 = X. The next black numeral is obliterated, but is readily restored, as X + 8 - 13 = V; V + 5 = X; X + 7 - 13 = IV. The next step presents a difficulty which we are unable to explain satisfactorily. The black numeral to be counted here, which stands over the animal figure in the upper division of Plate 39, is 12, both in Kingsborough's copy and in Förstemann's photograph, and is clear and distinct in each, and the following red numeral is as distinctly II, whereas IV + 12 - 13 = III. Moreover it is evident from the remaining numbers in the line that this red numeral should be II. We may assume that the Maya artist has made a mistake and written 12 instead of 11, which is evidently the number to be used in the count; but this arbitrary correction should not be resorted to so long as any other explanation is possible. From the fact that immediately under these numbers there are certain symbols which appear to have some reference to the termination of one year or cycle and the commencement of another, it is possible that a supplemental, unnumbered, but not uncounted day has been added. The fact that this interval of twelve days includes the day Ymix lends some probability to this supposition. Using 11 instead of 12, we continue our count as follows: IV + 11 - 13 = II; II + 5 = VII; VII + 8 - 13 = II; II + 11 = XIII. Thirteen is, therefore, the last number of the series, which is wanting in the codex.

The 8 and II next to the last pair of the series are not in line with the other numbers, but thrust into and near the bottom of the column of characters in the upper division of Plate 39. Adding together the black numbers as thus amended and restored, viz, 11, 8, 20, 13, 6, 20, 12, 19, 5, 1, 20, 12, 6, 8, 5, 7, 11, 5, 8, 11, the sum is found to be 208, which is a multiple of 13, and the final number of the series is 13. On the other hand, the sum of the series does not indicate the interval between the days of a column counting downwards, nor between two consecutive days or the corresponding days of two adjoining columns in any direction. The number of days from 13 Manik to 13 Chuen is 104, but counting 208 days from 13 Manik brings us to 13 Men, the third day of the first (left hand) column; 208 more to 13 Akbal, the fifth; 208 more to 13 Chuen, the second; and 208 more to 13 Cauac, the fourth, thus completing the column.

As these columns do not appear to form a continuous series it is possible they pertain to four different series of years, though the fact that each includes more than one year would seem to forbid this idea. It is more probable that they pertain to four different series, to each of which the line of numerals is to be considered as belonging.

The black numerals above the columns present a problem which I am unable to explain. The numbers stand in the original as follows:

1			
4	13	9	4
15	13	2	11

If we suppose that the lowest line denotes days, the one next above, months, and the uppermost, in which there is but a single number, years, the series will appear to be ascending toward the left, with the difference 4 months and 11 days, as shown by addition, thus:

Y.	M.	D.	
	4	11	Numbers over the fourth column.
	4	11	
	9	2	Numbers over the third column.
	4	1	
	13	13	Numbers over the second column.

Doubling the difference and adding we obtain the numbers over the first column:

Y.	M.	D.
	13	13
	9	2
1	4	15

What adds to the difficulty is the fact that if the columns are taken in reverse order the interval between the corresponding days is 4 months and 11 days; that is to say, counting from 13 Ix, first day of the fourth column, to 13 Chicchan, first day of the third column, we find the interval to be exactly 4 months and 11 days; and the same rule holds good throughout, so that reading across the upper line of days, from right to left, and following with the second line in the same way, ending with Akbal, the interval will be 4 months and 11 days between the consecutive days. Another significant fact is that by counting 4 months and 11 days from the first day of the year 1 Kan we reach 13 Ix; counting 9 months and 2 days from the same date brings us to 13 Chicchan; 13 months and 13 days, to 13 Cib; and 1 year and 4 days, to 13 Manik, which corresponds with the regular interval; it is therefore probable that there is an error in the numerals over the first or left hand column.

It is apparent from the illustrations given that in numeral series of the preceding type restorations can be made where not more than two numbers in succession are wanting. Even three can generally be restored if the numbers preceding and those following the break are distinct, but such restorations should be cautiously made.

In the middle division of Plate 9 is a short series where the number over the day column is wanting; moreover, there is uncertainty as to the number of days in the column and as to the signification of the red numerals, which are in pairs in Kingsborough's work instead of single as usual. Is it possible to explain these uncertainties and to reduce them to the usual simple form? Let us make the trial.

The days in the column are apparently the following: Ahau, Muluc, Ix, Cauac, Kan. The symbols, except that for Cauac, are too plain to admit of doubt, and there is no difficulty in reference to Cauac, the question of doubt being with regard to the Ahau, which is partially surrounded by other characters and may, apparently, be as correctly considered a part of the hieroglyphic inscription as of the day column.

Counting on the list of days in the calendar (Table II), as, for example, the Muluc column, we find the interval from Muluc to Ix is 5 days, from Ix to Cauac is 5 days, and from Cauac to Kan 5 days; but the interval from Ahau to Muluc is 9 days. From this fact we may reasonably infer that Ahau does not belong to the column. Moreover, the other 4 days are the four year bearers, and when they occur together the column usually consists of but 4 days, as, for example, in the lowest division of Plate 29 of this codex and Plate XXXII* of the Manuscript Troano. The numerals are 20; XIII, X; 20, XII, III; the number over the day column, as before stated, is wanting. The interval from 1 Muluc (or 2 or 3 Muluc) to Ix of the same number is 65 days. It is evident, therefore, that one of each pair of red numerals of the series given must be a counter and has been colored red by mistake. As the numbers in the last pair are III and XII, the number over the column must be 3 or 12. Suppose it is 12 and that XIII of the first pair is a counter, then XII + 20 + 13 - 13 - 13 - 13 = VI. As the number in the series is X this will not do. Supposing the X of the first pair of red numerals to be the counter, colored by mistake, the result is as follows: XII + 20 + 10 - 13 - 13 - 13 = III. This is also wrong, as the remainder should be XIII. Supposing the number over the column to be III and the XIII of the first pair and XII of the second to be the counters, the result agrees with the theory in every particular. Thus, III + 20 + 13 - 13 - 13 = X; X + 20 + 12 - 13 - 13 - 13 = III; and 20 + 13 + 20 + 12 = 65, the interval between 3 Muluc and 3 Ix. In Förstemann's copy the XIII and XII are black, thus verifying the conclusion here reached.

The series running through Plates 10c and 11c presents some difficulties which I have, so far, been unable to solve. The day columns and numerals are as follows:

I	XIII		
Ymix	Cimi	}	
Been	Ezanab		1, I; 5, VI; 10, III; 13, III; 15, V; 9 (?), XIII.
Chicchan	Oc		
Caban	Ik		
Muluc	Ix290-1		

The numerals in this case are very distinct, especially in the photographic copy, and there can be no doubt as to the days. Here the last black number, 9, is wrong; it should be 8, a fact noticed by Förstemann.290-2 Making this correction, the series is regular and consistent, so far as it relates to the right hand column, which has the red thirteen over it. But there is no series for the left hand column. Can it be that those who used the manuscript were expected to find the proper numbers by the line given? Possibly this is the reason the other series is not written out, as by adding one to each red number we obtain the proper result, which, if written out, would be as follows: 1, II; 5, VII; 10, IV; 13, IV; 15, VI; 3, I.

In Plate 30c are the four day columns here given, with the numeral eleven over each:

XI	XI	XI	XI
Ahau	Chicchan	Oc	Men
Caban	Ik	Manik	Eb
Ix	Cauac	Kan	Muluc
Chuen	Cib	Ymix	Cimi
Lamat	Been	Ezanab	Akbal.

Extending from the right of this group is a numeral series consisting of nine pairs of numbers, each pair the same, 13, XI. The sum of the black numbers (nine 13's) is 117 and the interval between the successive days of each column is 117; thus, from 11 Ahau to 11 Caban is 117 days, and so on down to Lamat, the last of the left hand column. From 11 Lamat to 11 Chicchan (first day of second column) is also 117, and so on to the end of the fourth column. These four columns, therefore, form one continuous series of 2,223 days, commencing with 11 Ahau and ending with 11 Akbal; but, by adding 117 days more, so as to bring us back to 11 Ahau—which appears to be in accordance with the plan of these series—the sum is 2,340 days, or nine cycles of 260 days each.291-1

The interval between the days, without reference to the numbers attached to them, is 17. It may be well to notice here the relation of the intervals between the days when counted in the two ways: (1) the apparent interval, or that which indicates their position in the month; (2) the true interval between the days, indicated by the symbols and numbers. When the first is 6 the latter, as we have found, is 20; when the first is 12 the latter is 52; when the first is 5 the latter is 65, and when it is 17 the latter is 117.

Particular attention is also called here to the fact that so far no indications of the use of the year period of 365 days have been observed; on the contrary the cycle of 260 days appears to be the period to which reference is chiefly made.

Attached to the day column in Plate 29c and running into 30c is a series which presents a difficulty I am unable to explain. The days and numerals in this case are as follows:

III		
Ix		
Cauac	}	16, VI; 16, IX; 16, XII; 16, (?)

Kan		
Muluc		

The red numeral over the day column is very distinctly III in Kingsborough's work, but is II, though somewhat blurred, in Förstemann's photograph. As III + 16 - 13 = VI, and the remaining numerals agree with this result, III must be correct. Adding together the pairs and casting out the thirteens, thus, III + 16 - 13 = VI; VI + 16 - 13 = IX; IX + 16 - 13 = XII; XII + 16 - 13 - 13 = II, we find the last red number, which is wanting in both copies of the codex, to be II, whereas, according to the theory advanced, it should be III. The sum of the black numerals (four 16's) is 64, while the interval between the days is 65. The only way of correcting the mistake, if one has been made, is by arbitrarily changing the last 16 to 17; but uniformity in the black numerals apparently forbids this change and and indicates that the variation from the usual rule must be accounted for in some other way.

In reference to this series, Dr. Förstemann292-1 remarks:

The column of the days has the difference 5; the fifth sign (in this case really superfluous), that of the thirteenth day, appears in a remarkable form, apparently as an inscription on a vessel. The black figures ought to give the sum 65, but we get only 4 × 16, or 64. But this appears to be merely an oversight by the copyist, for although in the Codex Troano, also, we find 64 several times instead of 65, still this has always appeared to me merely as a sign of the great negligence of the copyist of that manuscript.

Turning to the Manuscript Troano, Plate XXVIII*b, we find a column consisting of the four terminal days of the year, Been, Ezanab, Akbal, and Lamat, which of course have the same relation to one another as the first days. It is evident from the space that only four were intended to be given. The numerals in Brasseur's fac simile are XI; 20, 12, IV; 9, XIII; 10, X; 13, XI.

The red numeral over the column is XI, as is also the last of the series, but the sum of the black numbers is only 64, which would give X as the final number, as is evident from the following operation: XI + 32 - 13 - 13 - 13 = IV; IV + 9 = XIII; XIII + 10 - 13 = X; X + 13 - 13 = X. The interval between the days is 65. We have, therefore, precisely the same difficulty in this instance as in the case from the Dresden Codex under consideration. Moreover, the only method of correcting the mistake, if there is one, is by adding *one* to the last black number. It would be hazardous to assume that two mistakes, precisely the same in every respect, should have been made in regard to these exactly similar series. The probability that a mistake has been made is lessened by the fact that on Plate XXIX*b of the manuscript is another four day column, the last days of the years, as the preceding. The numeral over the column is XIII and the series is as follows: 13, XIII; 20, 18, XII; 13, XIII. Adding these and casting out the thirteens, we have this result: XIII + 13 - 13 = XIII; XIII + 20 + 18 - 13 - 13 - 13 = XII; XII + 13 - 13 = XII. This gives XII as the last number when it should be XIII. If a mistake has been made the only method of correcting it is by increasing the last black number by one, as in the other two cases alluded to.

It is proper to state that on the other hand there is another four day column on Plate XXXII*a of the last mentioned codex, the days of which are precisely the same as those on Plate 29c of the Dresden Codex, to wit, Ix, Cauac, Kan, Muluc. The numeral over it is XII and the series is as follows: 13, XII; 13, XII; 13, XII; 13, XII; 13, XII. This presents no difficulty, as it conforms in every respect to the rules given, but only serves to deepen the mystery in the other cases.

Going back to the series on Plate 29c of the Dresden Codex, we observe not only that the days of the column are the four year bearers, but also that one of the four cardinal symbols is found—in the superscription—in each of the four compartments through which the series extends. It is possible, therefore, that the series is intended to be applied separately to each of the four years. Supposing this to be the case, counting 64 days from 3 Ix would bring us to 2 Ezanab; 64 days from 3 Cauac to 2 Akbal; 64 days from 3 Kan to 2 Lamat; and 64 days from 3 Muluc to 2 Been. It is significant that in each case the day reached is that on which the given year terminates; for example, the Ix years (counting the five added days) terminate on Ezanab; the Cauac years on Akbal &c. If the intention was to have the series terminate with the end of the respective years, then these years must necessarily have been 2 Ix, 2 Cauac, 2 Kan, and 2 Muluc. I must confess that this explanation is not satisfactory; it is thrown out simply as a suggestion.

Running through the middle division of Plates 30 and 31 is this series:

3,	VIII	;	3,	VIII	;	3,	VIII	;	3,	VIII
5,	Oc		5,	Men		5,	Ahau		5,	Chicchan.

Commencing with 8 Oc (omitting for the present the 3 and 5 to the left) and counting thence 3 months and 5 days we reach 8 Men; 3 months and 5 days more and we reach 8 Ahau; 3 months and 5 days more bring us to 8 Chicchan, and 3 months and 5 days more bring us again to 8 Oc, thus completing a cycle of 260 days (13 months) and also accounting for the first pair of numerals—3 and 5 in the series. It appears to be a pretty general rule to commence a series of this type with the difference between the numbers of the series. One reason for this is apparent: that is, to complete the cycle of 260 days, to which most, if not all, of these groups appear to refer.

Dr. Förstemann says in regard to this line:293-1

This is the place where I first discovered how numbers of several figures are to be read; here for the first time I understood that the figure 3 with 5 below it is nothing but $3 \times 20 + 5$, or 65, and that they mean nothing else than the interval between the days, such as we have frequently met with so far; 4×65 is again the well known period of 260 days.

Plate 3 appears to be isolated and unfinished; at least it presents nothing on its face by which it can be directly connected with any other plate of the codex, notwithstanding the change made by Dr. Förstemann, by which 45 was brought next to it. The day column in this case is in the middle compartment of the upper division and consists of the following days: Ahau, Eb, Kan, Cib, Lamat; the red numeral over it is I. The numerals and days are arranged as follows:

(?)	(?)	4,	V(?)	15,	XIII
		I			
		Ahau			
8,	XIII	Eb			
		Kan			
		Cib			14 (?)
		Lamat			

As numerals belonging to two different series are never found in the same compartment it is fair to assume that those of the middle and right compartments pertain to one series. But what shall we say in reference to those in the left compartment, the upper pair of which is almost entirely obliterated? So far we have found no series extending to the left of the day column. Is this an exceptional case? I am inclined to believe it is, for the following reasons:

Taking the 4, V over the bird as the first pair of the series, we have I + 4 = V, which is so far correct; after this follows the pair in the lower left hand corner, 8, XIII, as V + 8 = XIII. It is probable that the obliterated pair in the upper left hand corner followed next, then the pair in the upper right hand corner, and last the partly obliterated one in the lower right hand corner. In this case the obliterated pair in the upper left hand corner should be 11, XI, as XIII + 11 - 13 = XI, and XI + 15 - 13 = XIII, and XIII + 14 - 13 - 13 = I, which makes the terminal red number of the series the same as that over the day column. This restoration requires no change of any of the numbers which can be distinctly read. By adding together the black numbers 4, 8, 11,

15, 14, the sum is found to be 52, precisely the interval between the days of the column. These facts are sufficient to render it more than probable that the restoration and the order as here given are correct. The series as thus given, including the number over the day column, is: I; 4, V; 8, XIII; 11, XI; 15, XIII; 14, I.

This is repeated, because on turning to Dr. Förstemann's comment on this series I find that he has restored and amended it so as to read thus: I; 10, XI; 4, V; 15, XIII; 9, XIII; 14, I; and he remarks that all would be plain sailing if, for the V before and the XIII after 15, we could read II and IV. This is true, but these numbers are too distinct to justify such change; moreover his "9" is not to be found on the page; it is true that the three dots over the line are not exactly spaced, but there are no indications of a fourth; the number is 8 and should, I think, be so read. His 10 is the obliterated black numeral; of course the value attributed to it depends upon the order given to the series. The fragments remaining of the red number of this pair I think warrant his making it XI.

Plates 46, 47, 48, 49, and 50 are peculiar and seemingly have no direct relation to any other part of the codex. In the upper left hand corner of each are four day columns, all more or less injured, but each column evidently contained, originally, thirteen days, or, more correctly speaking, the symbol for one day repeated thirteen times. In every case the day in the first (left hand) column and that in the third column are the same. As the numbers attached to them are absolutely unreadable in Kingsborough and much obliterated in the photograph, I give here restorations for the benefit of those studying this codex. This restoration is easily made by finding the order of the series, which can be obtained from Plates 49 and 50 of the photographic copy.

Plate 46:							
III	Cib.	II	Cimi.	V	Cib.	XIII	Kan.
XI	Cib.	X	Cimi.	XIII	Cib.	VIII	Kan.
VI	Cib.	V	Cimi.	VIII	Cib.	III	Kan.
I	Cib.	XIII	Cimi.	III	Cib.	XI	Kan.
IX	Cib.	VIII	Cimi.	XI	Cib.	VI	Kan.
IV	Cib.	III	Cimi.	VI	Cib.	I	Kan.
XII	Cib.	XI	Cimi.	I	Cib.	IX	Kan.
VII	Cib.	VI	Cimi.	IX	Cib.	IV	Kan.
II	Cib.	I	Cimi.	IV	Cib.	XII	Kan.

X	Cib.	IX	Cimi.	XII	Cib.	VII	Kan.
V	Cib.	IV	Cimi.	VII	Cib.	II	Kan.
XIII	Cib.	XII	Cimi.	II	Cib.	X	Kan.
VIII	Cib.	VII	Cimi.	X	Cib.	V	Kan.

Plate 47:

II	Ahau.	I	Oc.	IV	Ahau.	XII	Lamat.
X	Ahau.	IX	Oc.	XII	Ahau.	VII	Lamat.
V	Ahau.	IV	Oc.	VII	Ahau.	II	Lamat.
XIII	Ahau.	XII	Oc.	II	Ahau.	X	Lamat.
VIII	Ahau.	VII	Oc.	X	Ahau.	V	Lamat.
III	Ahau.	II	Oc.	V	Ahau.	XIII	Lamat.
XI	Ahau.	X	Oc.	XIII	Ahau.	VIII	Lamat.
VI	Ahau.	V	Oc.	VIII	Ahau.	III	Lamat.
I	Ahau.	XIII	Oc.	III	Ahau.	XI	Lamat.
IX	Ahau.	VIII	Oc.	XI	Ahau.	VI	Lamat.
IV	Ahau.	III	Oc.	VI	Ahau.	I	Lamat.
XII	Ahau.	XI	Oc.	I	Ahau.	IX	Lamat.
VII	Ahau.	VI	Oc.	IX	Ahau.	IV	Lamat.

As the arrangement and the order of the series are readily seen from the two examples given, only the top and bottom lines of the remaining series will be presented.

Plate 48:							
I	Kan.	XIII	Ix.	III	Kan.	XI	Eb.
*	*	*	*	*	*	*	*
VI	Kan.	V	Ix.	VIII	Kan.	III	Eb.
Plate 49:							
XIII	Lamat.	XII	Ezanab.	II	Lamat.	X	Cib.
*	*	*	*	*	*	*	*
V	Lamat.	IV	Ezanab.	VII	Lamat.	II	Cib.

Plate 50:							
XII	Eb.	XI	Ik.	I	Eb.	IX	Ahau.
*	*	*	*	*	*	*	*
IV	Eb.	III	Ik.	VI	Eb.	I	Ahau.

A careful examination of these groups will bring to light the following relations of the numbers, days, columns, and series to one another:

The numerals of any one column, counting downwards, differ from one another by 8; that is to say, by adding 8 to any one and casting out 13 when the sum exceeds that number, the next lower number will be obtained; or, reversing the operation and counting upward, the difference is found to be 5. The true interval between the days of the columns (counting downwards) is 3 months (60 days), a rule which holds good as to all the series and each column. Thus, from 3 Cib to 11 Cib is 3 months, or 60 days; from 11 Cib to 6 Cib, 3 months; from 2 Cimi to 10 Cimi, 3 months, and from 13 Kan to 8 Kan, 3 months.

Counting on the list of the days of the month, without reference to the week numbers attached to them, it will be found that from Cib to Cimi is an interval of 10 days, and from Cib to Kan is an interval of 8 days. This rule holds good as to all the series, showing that all are arranged upon precisely the same plan. The true interval between any day of the first column of either series (the week number attached being considered) and the opposite or corresponding day in the second column, is 4 months and 10 days, that between the corresponding days of the second and third columns is 12 months and 10 days, that between the days of the third and fourth columns is 8 days, and that between the corresponding days of the fourth or last column of one series or plate and the first column of the following series or plate (taking the plates in the order they are paged) is 11 months and 16 days.

In order to illustrate this we will run through the lowest line of each series, taking them in the order of the pages.296-1

These are as follows:

Plate 46:	VIII	Cib.	VII	Cimi.	X	Cib.	V	Kan.
Plate 47:	VII	Ahau.	VI	Oc.	IX	Ahau.	IV	Lamat.
Plate 48:	VI	Kan.	V	Ix.	VIII	Kan.	III	Eb.

Plate 49:	V	Lamat.	IV	Ezanab.	VII	Lamat.	II	Cib.
Plate 50:	IV	Eb.	III	Ik.	VI	Eb.	I	Ahau.

FIG 362. Copy of Plate 50, Dresden Codex.

By counting on the calendar (our Table II), as heretofore explained, the reader will observe that the interval from 8 Cib to 7 Cimi is 4 months and 10 days; from 7 Cimi to 10 Cib is 12 months and 10 days; from 10 Cib to 5 Kan is 8 days; from 5 Kan to 7 Ahau is 11 months and 16 days; from 7 Ahau to 6 Oc, 4 months and 10 days; from 6 Oc to 9 Ahau, 12 months and 10 days; from 9 Ahau to 4 Lamat, 8 days; from 4 Lamat to 6 Kan, 11 months and 16 days, and so on to the end of the series on Plate 50. Referring to the codex the reader will observe at the bottom of each plate and directly under—that is to say, in the same vertical lines as the day columns—two lines of red numerals. It is impossible to determine these in Kingsborough's copy (except on Plate 50), but they can readily be made out on the photographed plates. (See the copy of Plate 50, given in Fig. 362.) Those on a single plate are as follows:

{	XI,	IV,	XII,	0,
	XVI,	X,	X,	VIII.

The 0 here represents a red, diamond shaped symbol.

If the upper line represents months and the lower line days, these numbers will indicate the intervals between the columns and are properly placed. For example, the XI and XVI signify 11 months and 16 days, the interval between the last column of the preceding plate and the first column of the plate on which they stand; the IV and X, the interval of 4 months and 10 days between the first and second columns; XII and X, the interval of 12 months and 10 days between the second and third columns; and 0, VIII, the interval of 8 days between the third and fourth columns. It is apparent from this that the red, diamond shaped symbol represented by 0 over the VIII denotes a cipher or nought, a conclusion reached independently by Förstemann.

If this supposition as to the arrangement of the series and the signification of these numbers be correct, it is apparent that the plates are to be taken in the order in which they are paged, that is, from left to right, as the others so far noticed, an inference borne out by another fact now to be mentioned.

Immediately below each of these four column day series are four lines of characters (hieroglyphics), and immediately under the latter three horizontal lines of black numerals, with here and there a red, diamond shaped symbol inserted. As these numerals stand directly in the vertical lines of the day columns, it is possible the two have some connection with each other, a supposition somewhat strengthened by what has been observed in regard to the red numerals at the bottom of the plates. To test this and also for the reason that we propose to discuss their relations and their use, we give here the bottom line of days of each of the five series (or plates), together with their week numbers attached; also, the numbers of the three lines of black numerals mentioned, taking them in the order of the paging as here shown:

Plate 46:				
	VIII Cib.	VII Cimi.	X Cib.	V Kan.
			1	1
	11	16	10	11
	16	6	16	4
Plate 47:				

VII Ahau.	VI Oc.	IX Ahau.	IV Lamat.
2	2	3	3
5	9	4	4
0	10	0	8

Plate 48:

VI Kan.	V Ix.	III Kan.	III Eb.
3	4	4	4
16	2	15	15
3(?)	14	4	12

Plate 49:

V Lamat.	IV Ezanab.	VII Lamat.	II Cib.
5	5	6	6
9	13	8	8
8	18	8	16

Plate 50:

IV Eb.	III Ik.	VI Eb.	1 Ahau.
7	7	8	8
3	7	1	2
12	2	12	0

In considering these horizontal lines it is to be understood that the series runs through the five pages, 46-50.

Let us proceed upon the supposition that the figures of the lowest of the three lines denote days of the month, the numbers of the middle line months, and those of the upper line years. As already shown, the interval between 8 Cib and 7 Cimi is 4 months and 10 days; adding 4 months and 10 days to 11 months and 16 days (bearing in mind that 20 days make a month and 18 months a year), the sum is found to be 16 months and 6 days, precisely the figures under 7 Cimi. As already ascertained, the interval between 7 Cimi and 10 Cib is 12 months and 10 days; this added to 16 months and 6 days gives

1 year, 10 months, 16 days, precisely the figures under 10 Cib. The interval between 10 Cib and 5 Kan is 8 days; this added to the 1 year, 10 months, and 16 days gives 1 year, 11 months, and 4 days, the figures under 5 Kan. The interval between 5 Kan and 7 Ahau is 11 months, 16 days, which, added to the preceding, gives 2 years, 5 months, 0 day, agreeing with the figures under 7 Ahau, if the symbol represented by 0 signifies nought. That this rule holds good throughout the entire series, by making one correction, is shown by the following additions:

Years.	Months.	Days.		
	11	16		Under VIII Cib, Plate 46.
	4	10		
	16	6		Under VII Cimi, Plate 46.
	12	10		
1	10	16		Under X Cib, Plate 46.
		8		
1	11	4		Under V Kan, Plate 46.
	11	16		
2	5	0		Under VII Ahau, Plate 47.
	4	10		
2	9	10		Under VI Oc, Plate 47.
	12	10		
3	4	0		Under IX Ahau, Plate 47.
		8		
3	4	8		Under IV Lamat, Plate 47.
	11	16		
3	16	4	300-1	Under VI Kan, Plate 48.
	4	10		
4	2	14		Under V Ix, Plate 48.
	12	10		
4	15	4		Under VIII Kan, Plate 48.

				8			
4		15		12			Under III Eb, Plate 48.
		11		16			
5		9		8			Under V Lamat, Plate 49.
		4		10			
5		13		18			Under IV Ezanab, Plate 49.
		12		10			
6		8		8			Under VII Lamat, Plate 49.
				8			
6		8		16			Under II Cib, Plate 49.
		11		16			
7		2		12			Under IV Eb, Plate 50.
		4		10			
7		7		2			Under III Ik, Plate 50.
		12		10			
8		1		12			Under VI Eb, Plate 50.
				8			
8		2		0			Under I Ahau, Plate 50.

The proof of the correctness of the theory advanced may, therefore, be considered conclusive, as it amounts, in fact, to a mathematical demonstration.

Dr. Förstemann, who considers these lines of black numbers, standing one above another, as representing different grades of units—thus, the lowest, single units; the second, units twenty-fold the lower; the third, eighteen-fold the second; the fourth, twenty-fold the third, &c.—has found the correct intervals of the series, which he states are 236, 90, 250, and 8 days, agreeing with our 11 months, 16 days; 4 months, 10 days; 12 months, 10 days, and 8 days.

As all the discoveries mentioned herein were made previous to the receipt of Dr. Förstemann's work, I give them according to my own method, acknowledging any modification due to his work. Although I shall compare special results from time to time, an explanation of Dr. Förstemann's method is reserved for a future paper, as his work was not received until I was revising my notes for publication.

The foregoing explanation of the series shows it to be very simple and makes it clear that it relates to the day columns at the top of the pages. Still, there is one point somewhat difficult to understand. Are the numbers of the third or lowest line intended to denote the positions in the month of the days in the columns above? If so, the month must have commenced with Ymix, as can readily be shown in the following manner:

TABLE III.

1.	Ymix.
2.	Ik.
3.	Akbal.
4.	Kan.
5.	Chicchan.
6.	Cimi.
7.	Manik.
8.	Lamat.
9.	Muluc.
10.	Oc.
11.	Chuen.
12.	Eb.
13.	Been.
14.	Ix.
15.	Men.
16.	Cib.
17.	Caban.
18.	Ezanab.
19.	Cauac.
20.	Ahau.

If we write in a column in proper order the 20 days of the Maya month, commencing with Ymix, and number them consecutively, as in Table III, we

- 47 -

shall find by comparison that the numbers in the lower line indicate the position, in this column, of the days directly over them. Take, for example, the lower line of black numerals on Plate 46, writing over them the respective days of the columns, thus:

Cib.	Cimi.	Cib.	Kan.
16	6	16	4

Referring to Table III we see that Cib is the sixteenth day, Cimi the sixth, and Kan the fourth.

The days and numbers of Plate 47 are:

Ahau.	Oc.	Ahau.	Lamat.
0	10	0	8

Ahau is the twentieth day—here is the diamond shaped symbol—Oc is the tenth, and Lamat the eighth, and so on to the end of the series on Plate 50.

It may be justly argued that such relation to some given day of the month would necessarily follow in any series of this kind made up by adding together intervals of days and months. Still it is not at all likely that these series were made up without reference to fitted and determinable dates. If so, the months given must be months of certain determinable years, and the days denoted must be days of particular months. In other words, if we had the proper starting point we should be able to determine the position in the calendar of any day or month mentioned in the series.

First. It is easily seen by reference to the calendar (Table II) that Cib is not the sixteenth day of the month of any of the four years, nor is Cimi the sixth nor Kan the fourth. The idea that the figures of this lower line represent the days of the month must, therefore, be given up unless we assume that the year commenced with Ymix. It may be worthy of notice at this point that the list of days on the so-called "title page" of the Manuscript Troano begins with Ymix. It is also true that the remarkable quadruple series in the Codex Cortesianus on Plates 13-18 commences with Ymix; as this is evidently some kind of a calendar table, its bearing on the question now before us is important.

Second. It can easily be shown that the months referred to in the series, if the numbers given denote specific months, are not those of the Kan years. The first, 8 Cib, if in the eleventh month, must be in the year 4 Kan; counting forward from this 4 months and 10 days to 7 Cimi brings us into the sixteenth month of the year 4 Kan; this agrees with our figures on Plate 46. Counting forward 12 months and 10 days to 10 Cib, we reach the tenth month of the next year; 8 days more carry us to the eleventh month, which still agrees with the figures in the codex. Counting 11 months and 16 days more to 7 Ahau, we reach but do not pass the fourth month of the next year; hence the result does not correspond with the series, which has at this point a 5 in the middle line. The same will be found true in regard to the other years as given in our calendar (Table II). This result, as a matter of course, must follow if the figures in the lower line of the series do not denote the month days of some one of the year series as usually given.

Another fact also becomes apparent here, viz, that the 5 supplemental days of the year are not brought into the count, the year consisting throughout of 360 days. There is, in fact, nothing here indicating the four year series as given in the authorities and as represented in our calendar table; yet this ought to appear wherever a series extends over more than one year.

Dr. Förstemann says that this entire series of black numerals covers 2,920 days, or 8 years of 365 days. This is true, but the concluding figures show that it is given by the writer of the codex as 8 years and 2 months, which would also be 2,920 days, counting the years at 360 days each and the months 20 days each; moreover, the members of the series are based throughout upon the year of 360 days. His theory that the intervals of the series relate to the movements of the planet Venus is, as yet, a mere hypothesis, which needs further proof before it can demand acceptance; but his discovery of the methods of identifying the month symbols on the five plates now under consideration is important. Although I had noticed that most of the characters which he mentions are month symbols, I did not succeed in identifying all of them.

According to his conclusion, which appears to be justified not only by the evidence he gives but by an additional fact that I shall, presently mention, there are four of these symbols in the upper row of the middle group of written characters on each plate and four in the upper and lower lines of the lower group on each plate (see, for example, Fig. 362). Each of these symbols (except three or four) has a black number attached to it which denotes the day of the month represented by the symbol.

These months and days as given by Dr. Förstemann are as follows, the positions of the lines as here given corresponding with those of the plates:

TABLE IV.—*Table showing months and days.*

	Month.	Day.	Month.	Day.	Month.	Day.	Month.	Day.
Plate 46	7	4	11	14	5	19	6	7
	11	8	15	18	10	4	10	12

	1	14	6	4	18	14	1	2
Plate 47	18	3	4	8	16	18	17	6
	4	3	8	13	2	18	3(not 2)	6
	10	10	15	3	9	8	9	16
Plate 48	10	17	15	7	9	12	10	20
	15	2	1	7	13	17	14	5
	3	7	7	17	2	2	2	10
Plate 49	3	11	8	1	2	6	2	14
	7	16	12	6	6	11	6	19
	14	6	18	16	13	1	13	9
Plate 50	14	10	18	20	13	5	13	13
	18	15	5	20	17	10	17	18
	6	20	11	10	5	15	6	3

An examination of the plates will show that Dr. Förstemann has filled out the following obliterated or wanting day numbers, to wit, the first of the upper line of Plate 46, the fourth of the upper line of Plate 47, and the second of the middle line and first of the lower line of Plate 50. He has also ventured to change the first day number of the lower line of Plate 46 from 16 to 14. Where the number 20 is found in his list there is no corresponding number in the codex, the month symbol only being given. It is evident he has proceeded in these cases upon the theory that the absence of a number indicated that the month was completed. Although probably correct in this conclusion, the question will arise, Does the symbol in such cases denote the *month completed* or the *month reached?*

The intervals between these dates are as follows, the left hand column being those between the first and second columns of Förstemann's list (our Table IV), the second column those between the second and third columns of his list, the third column those between the third and fourth columns of his list, and the fourth column those between the last date of one plate and the first of the next:

TABLE V.—*Table showing intervals between dates.*

	Month.	Day.		Month.	Day.		Month.	Day.		Month.	Day.	
Plate 46	4	10		12	5		0	8		11	16	
	4	10		12	6	b	0	8		11	11	
	4	10		12	10		0	8		9	8	d
Plate 47	4	5		12	10		0	8		11	11	
	4	10		12	5		0	8	c	11	16	e
	4	13	a	12	5		0	8		11	11	
Plate 48	4	10		12	5			8		11	11	
	4	5		12	10		0	8		11	11	
	4	10		12	5		0	8		11	16	
Plate 49	4	10		12	5		0	8		11	16	
	4	10		12	5		0	8		11	16	
	4	10		12	5		0	8		11	11	
Plate 50	4	10		12	5		0	8		11	11	
	4	5		12	10		0	8		11	10	
	4	10		12	5		0	8		12	11	g

Although it is apparent that the variations from the intervals of the black numeral and day series above them are too numerous and too uniform to be considered mistakes, yet there is little reason to doubt that these month numbers are connected with and depend upon the day series given in the columns above.

That there are some errors is quite clear; for instance, the variation at *a* arises from the fact that Dr. Förstemann gives the date here as 10 months, 10 days, whereas the codex has it 10 months, 13 days. Making this correction the interval will be 4 months, 10 days. The correction will make the interval at *d* 9, 11, instead of 9, 8. Still there is a variation of two months from the usual interval, which, if corrected on the supposition that Dr. Förstemann has mistaken the month, would necessitate a change of the remainder of the series given in this line. The interval at *c*, according to the figure given by Dr. Förstemann, would be retrograde, that is, minus 12. This arises from the fact that he gives the last date in the middle line on Plate 47 as 2 months, 6 days, whereas the symbol is very distinctly that of the third month, and the eight day series is unbroken if this correction is made.

When these evident errors are corrected the series of intervals show very clearly a system and periodicity depending on the day column series in the upper part of the pages. In the first column (Table V) the interval is usually 4 months, 10 days, precisely the same as between the first and second day columns, but occasionally it is 4 months, 5 days, which will still bring it to one of the four day series, including the day indicated by the date—4 months, 10 days. This will be understood by examining our calendar (Table II). The corresponding days in the four year columns were, by the Maya system, necessarily brought together in the calendar; for example, they are arranged in the series pictured on Plates 13-18 of the Cortesian Codex precisely as given in our Table II. This skip of five days is also apparent in the second and fourth columns of differences (Table V). Whether Dr. Förstemann is correct in all his identifications of months among the symbols on the five plates now under consideration is a question I feel unqualified to answer without a much more careful comparison and study of these characters than I have given them.

Running through the upper division of Plates 53 to 58 and continued through the lower division of Plates 51 to 58—that is to say, commencing in the upper division of 53 and running into 58, then back to the lower division of 51 and ending in 58—is a remarkable compound series. It consists, first, of a three line series of black numerals standing above; second, a middle series of short, three day columns, or columns each of three day symbols, with red numerals attached; and, third, below, a two line series of numerals, those of the upper line red and of the lower black numbers.

As this series is a very important one in the study of the relations of the numerals to one another and to the days indicated, an exact copy of it is given in Figs. 363-370, each figure representing a page and the whole standing in the same order as in the original. The red numerals and red symbols are, as usual, given in outline as an indication of their color.

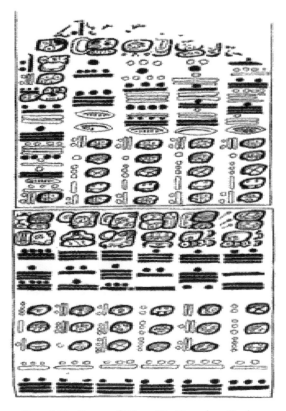

FIG. 363. Copy of Plate 51, Dresden Codex.

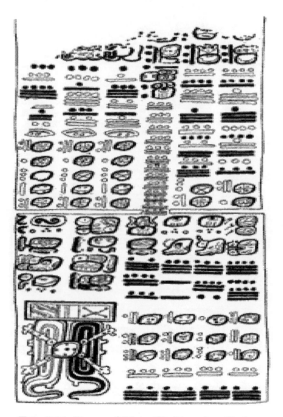

FIG. 364. Copy of Plate 52, Dresden Codex.

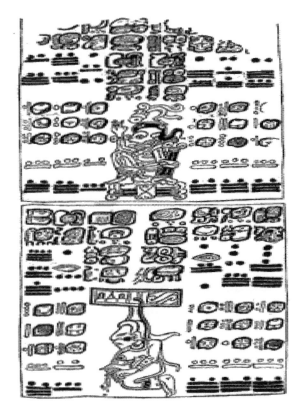

FIG. 365. Copy of Plate 55, Dresden Codex.

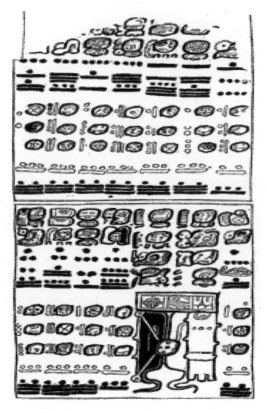

FIG. 366. Copy of Plate 54, Dresden Codex.

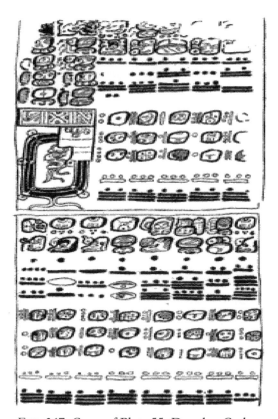

FIG. 367. Copy of Plate 55, Dresden Codex.

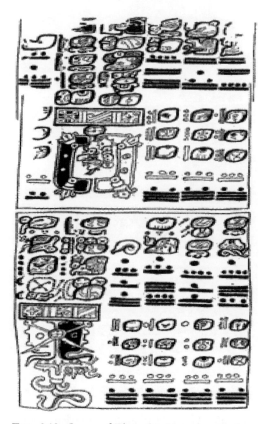

FIG. 368. Copy of Plate 56, Dresden Codex.

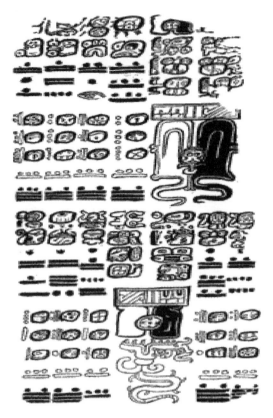

FIG. 369. Copy of Plate 57, Dresden Codex.

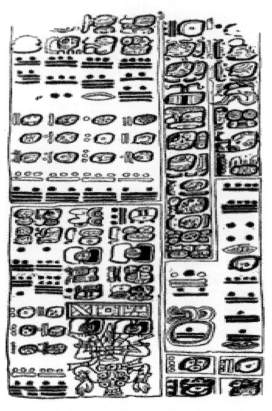

FIG. 370. Copy of Plate 58, Dresden Codex.

In order to assist those not familiar with the numeral and day symbols, the entire series is given in the following tables in names and Arabic and Roman numerals, as usual. The obliterated symbols and numbers are restored.

TABLE VI.—*Table of numeral and day symbols.* (Plate 51*b*.)

	14		15		15		16		16		17
	16		7		16		7		16		5
	14		11		8		5		2		10
IV	Ik.	XII	Cauac.	VII	Cib.	II	Been.	X	Oc.	II	Ezanab.
V	Akbal.	XIII	Ahau.	VIII	Caban.	III	Ix	XI	Chuen	III	Cauac.
VI	Kan.	I	Ymix.	IX	Ezanab.	IV	Men.	XII	Eb.	IV	Ahau.VI-1
	VIII		VIII		VIII		VIII		VIII		VII
	17		17		17		17		17		8
VI-1 The symbol in this case is that of Been, but this is a manifest error, as Ahau follows Cauac.

- 60 -

TABLE VII.—*Table of numeral and day symbols.* (Plate 52*b*.)

	17	18	18	19
	14	5	14	4
	8	5	2	19
	XI Cib.	VI Been.	I Oc.	IX Manik.
[Picture.]	XII Caban.	VII Ix.	II Chuen.	X Lamat.
	XIII Ezanab.	VIII Men.	III Eb.	XI Muluc.
	VIII	VIII	VIII	VIII
	17? (18)VII-1	17	17	17

VII-1 The variation from the rule found here is explained a little further on.

TABLE VIII.—*Table of numeral and day symbols.* (Plate 53*a*.)

		1		1	2	2
7	17	7		15	6	15
17	18	2		14?(19)VIII-1	16	13
VI Kan.	I Ymix.	VI Muluc.	[Picture.]	I Cimi.	IX Akbal.	IV Ahau.
VII Chicchan.	II Ik.	VII Oc.		II Manik.	X Kan.	V Ymix.
VIII Cimi.	III Akbal.	VIII Chuen.		III Lamat.	XI Chicchan.	VI Ik.
VIII	VIII	VII		VIII	VIII	VIII
17	17	8		17	17	17

VIII-1 The 14 here is manifestly an error, one of the lines in the number symbol having been omitted; it should be 19.

TABLE IX.—*Table of numeral and day symbols.* (Plate 53*b*.)

	1		1	1	1
19	0		0	1	1
13	3		12	2	11
16	4		1	18	15
IV Kan.	IX Eb.	[Picture.]	IV Muluc.	XII Cimi.	VII Akbal.
V Chicchan.	X Been.		V Oc.	XIII Manik.	VIII Kan.
VI Cimi.	XI Ix.		VI Chuen.	I Lamat.	IX Chicchan.
VIII	VII		VIII	VIII	VIII
17	8		17	17	17

TABLE X.—*Table of numeral and day symbols.* (Plate 54*a*.)

3	3	4	4	5	5	6
6	15	6	15	5	10	4
11	8	5	5	19	16	4
XIII Ezanab.	VIII Men.	III Eb.	XI Muluc.	VI Cib.	I Akbal.	VI Chuen.
I Cauac.	IX Cib.	IV Been.	XII Oc.	VII Caban.	II Kan.	VII Eb.
II Ahau.	X Caban.	V Ix.	XIII Chuen.	VIII Ezanab.	III Chicchan.	VIII Been.
VIII	VIII	VIII	VIII	VIII	VIII	VII
17	17	17	17	17	17	8

TABLE XI.—*Table of numeral and day symbols.* (Plate 54*b*.)

1	1	1	1		1
2	2	3	3		4
2	11	2	9		0XI-1

12	9	6	14		11
II Ahau.	X Caban.	V Ix.	X Ik.	[Picture]	V Cauac.
III Ymix.	XI Ezanab.	VI Men.	XI Akbal.		VI Ahau.
IV Ik.	XII Cauac.	VII Cib.	XII Kan.		VII Ymix.
VIII	VIII	VIII	VII		VIIXI-2
17	17	17	8		17

XI-1 The 0 inserted at various points in these tables denotes as usual the red, diamond shaped symbol, which apparently signifies "nought."

XI-2 The numeral symbol in this case, both in Kingsborough's copy and in the photograph, is VII, one dot having been omitted by a mistake of the original artist.

TABLE XII.—*Table of numeral and day symbols.* (Plate 55*a.*)

	8	7	7	8	8
	13	3	12	3	12
	2	18	16	13	10
	II Muluc.XII-1	X Cimi.	V Akbal.	XIII Ahau.	VIII Caban.
[Picture]	III Oc.	XI Manik.	VI Kan.	I Ymix.	IX Ezanab.
	IV Chuen.	XII Lamat.	VII Chicchan.	II Ik.	X Cauac.
	VIII	VIII	VIII	VIII	VIII
	17	17	17	17	17

XII-1 In Kingsborough's work the symbol in this case is that of Been, but should be Muluc, as it is in the photograph.

TABLE XIII.—*Table of numeral and day symbols.* (Plate 55*b*.)

1	1	1	1	1	1	1	1
4	5	5	6	6	6	7	7
9	0	9	0	8	17	8	15
8	6	3	0	17	14	11	19
XIII Cib.	IX Ix.	IV Chuen.	XII Lamat.	VII Chicchan.	II Ik.	X Cauac.	II Manik.
I Caban.	X Men.	V Eb.	XIII Muluc.	VIII Cimi.	III Akbal.	XI Ahau.	III Lamat.
II Ezanab.	XI Cib.	VI Been.	I Oc.	IX Manik.	IV Kan.	XII Ymix.	IV Muluc.
VIII	VIII	VIII	VIII	VIII	VIII	VIII	VII
17	17?(18)	17	17	17	17	17	8

TABLE XIV.—*Table of numeral and day symbols.* (Plate 56*a*.)

9		9	10	10
1		10	1	10
18		15	12	9
XIII Chicchan.		VIII Ik.	III Cauac.	XI Cib.
I Cimi.	[Picture]	IX Akbal.	IV Ahau.	XII Caban.
II Manik.		X Kan.	V Ymix.	XIII Ezanab.
VII		VIII	VIII	VIII
8		17	17	17

TABLE XV.—*Table of numeral and day symbols.* (Plate 56*b*.)

	1	1	1	1
	8	8	9	9
	6	15	6	15
	16	14	11	8
[Picture]	X Kan.	VI Ik.	I Cauac.	IX Cib.

XI Chicchan.	VII Akbal.	II Ahau.	X Caban.
XII Cimi.	VIII Kan.	III Ymix.	XI Ezanab.
VIII	VIII	VIII	VIII
17	17?(8)	17	17

TABLE XVI.—*Table of numeral and day symbols.* (Plate 57*a*.)

11	11	12	12	
1	10	1	8	
6	4	0	8	
VII Ix.	II Chuen.	X Lamat.	II Cib.	
VIII Men.	III Eb.	XI Muluc.	III Caban.	[Picture]
IX Cib.	IV Been.	XII Oc.	IV Ezanab.	
VIII	VIII	VIII	VIIIXVI-1	
17	17	17	17XVI-2	

XVI-1 This should be VII.

XVI-2 This should be 8.

TABLE XVII.—*Table of numeral and day symbols.* (Plate 57*b*.)

1	1	1		1	1
10	10	11		11	12
6	15	4		13	4
5	2	10		7	4
IV Been.	XII Oc.	IV Ezanab.	[Picture]	XII Men.	VII Eb.
V Ix.	XIII Chuen.	V Cauac.		XIII Cib.	VIII Been.
VI Men.	I Eb.	VI Ahau.		I Caban.	IX Ix.

VIII	VIII	VII		VIII	VIII
17	17	8		17	17

TABLE XVIII.—*Table of numeral and day symbols.* (Plate 58*a*.)

12	13	13	14
17	8	17	7
5	2	0	17
X Been.	V Oc.	I Lamat.	II Chicchan.
XI Ix.	VI Chuen.	II Muluc.	X Cimi.
XII Men.	VII Eb.	III Oc.	XI Manik.
VIII	VIII	VIII	VIII
17	17	17	17

TABLE XIX.—*Table of numeral and day symbols.* (Plate 58*b*.)

1	1	
12	13	
13	3	
1	18	
II Muluc.	X Cimi.	[Picture.]
III Oc.	XI Manik.	
IV Chuen.	XII Lamat.	
VIII	VIII	
17	17	

The spaces in the lists indicate the positions of the pictures of persons and curtain-like ornaments inserted here and there, as seen in Figs. 363-370.

In order to explain this series, we commence with that portion of it found in the lower division of Plate 51 (Fig. 363).

Omitting any reference for the present to the black numbers over the day columns, we call attention first to the days and to the red numerals attached to them. Those in the division selected as an illustration are as follows:

IV	Ik.	XII	Cauac.	VII	Cib.	II	Been.	X	Oc.	II	Ezanab.
V	Akbal.	XIII	Ahau.	VIII	Caban.	III	Ix.	XI	Chuen.	III	Cauac.
VI	Kan.	I	Ymix.	IX	Ezanab.	IV	Men.	XII	Eb.	IV	Ahau.317-1

It will be observed that the week numbers of the days in each single column follow one another in regular arithmetical order, thus: in the first column, 4, 5, 6; in the second, 12, 13, 1; in the third, 7, 8, 9; and so on throughout the entire series. The interval, therefore, between the successive days of a column is 1; or, in other words, the days follow one another in regular order, as in the month series, so that having the first day of a column given we know at once the other two. It is apparent, therefore, that the intervals between the three correspondingly opposite days of any two associate columns are the same; that is to say, the interval between 5 Akbal and 13 Ahau, in the first two columns given above is the same as that between 4 Ik and 12 Cauac, and also as that between 6 Kan and 1 Ymix. This is also true if the attached week numbers are omitted; for instance, the interval between Ik and Cauac, counting on the list of days forming the month, is 17 days, and it is the same between Kan and Ymix. Taking the second and third columns we find here the same interval. This holds good in that part of the series above given until we reach the last two columns; here the interval between Oc and Ezanab is 8 days and it is the same between the other days of these two columns.

This being ascertained, the next step is to determine the true interval between the first days of these columns, taking the numbers attached to them into consideration. Referring to our calendar (Table II) and (for reasons which will be given hereafter) using the Muluc column and counting from 4 Ik, as heretofore explained, we find the interval between this and 12 Cauac to be 8 months and 17 days; counting in the same way from 12 Cauac, 8 months and 17 days more bring us to 7 Cib; 8 months and 17 days more to 10 Oc. So far the intervals have been the same; but at this point we find a variation from the rule, as the interval between 10 Oc and 2 Ezanab (first of the next column) is 7 months and 8 days.

These intervals furnish the explanation of the red and black numerals below the day columns.

These numerals, as the reader will observe by reference to Fig. 363 or the written interpretation thereof in Table VI, are 8 and 17 under the first five columns, but 7 and 8 under the sixth column, the red (8 under the first five and 7 under the sixth) indicating the months and the black (17 under the first five and 8 under the sixth) the days of the intervals. This holds good throughout all that portion of the series running through the lower divisions of Plates 51 to 58, with three exceptions, which will now be pointed out.

In order to do this it will be necessary to repeat here a part of the series on Plate 51*b* and part of that on Plate 52*b*; that is, the two right hand columns of the former and the two left hand columns of the latter, between which is the singular picture shown in the *lower left hand corner* of our Fig. 364:

Plate 51*b*.			Plate 52*b*.	
X Oc.	II Ezanab.		XI Cib.	VI Been.
XI Chuen.	III Cauac.		XII Caban.	VII Ix.
XII Eb.	IV Ahau.	[Picture.]	XIII Ezanab.	VIII Men.
VIII	VII		VIII	VIII
17	8		17	17

As before stated, the interval between 10 Oc and 2 Ezanab is 7 months and 8 days, as indicated by the red and black numerals under the latter. According to the red and black numbers under the column commencing with 11 Cib, the interval between 2 Ezanab and 11 Cib should be 8 months and 17 days, the usual difference, when, in fact, as we see by counting on the calendar, it is 8 months and 18 days. That this variation cannot be attributed to a mistake on the part of the author or of the artist is evident from the fact that the interval between 11 Cib and 6 Been (first of the next column) is 8 months and 17 days and that the difference throughout the rest of the series follows the rule given; that is to say, each is 8 months and 17 days, except at two other points where this variation is found and at the regular intervals where the difference of 7 months and 8 days occurs.319-1 Precisely the same variation occurs on Plate 55*b* in passing from the first to the second column and on Plate 56*b* between columns 1 and 2.

Why these singular exceptions? It is difficult, if not impossible, for us, with our still imperfect knowledge of the calendar system formerly in vogue among the Mayas, to give a satisfactory answer to this question. But we reserve further notice of it until other parts of the series have been explained.

Reference will now be made to the three lines of black numerals immediately above the day columns. Still confining our examinations to the lower divisions, the reader's attention is directed to these lines, as given in Tables VI, VII, IX, XI, XIII, XV, XVII, and XIX. As there are three numbers in each short column we take for granted, judging by what has been shown in regard to the series on Plates 46-50, that the lowest of the three denotes days, the middle months, and the upper years, and that the intervals are the same between these columns as between the day columns under them. The correctness of this supposition is shown by the following additions: Starting with the first or left hand column on Plate 51*b*, we add successively the differences indicated by the corresponding red and black numbers under the day columns. If this gives in each case (save the two or three exceptions heretofore referred to) the numbers in the next column to the right throughout the series, the demonstration will be complete.

Years.	Months.	Days.		
14	16	14		First column on Plate 51*b*.
	8	17		
15	7	11		Second column on Plate 51*b*.
	8	17		
15	16	8		Third column on Plate 51*b*.
	8	17		
16	7	5		Fourth column on Plate 51*b*.
	8	17		
16	16	2		Fifth column on Plate 51*b*.
	7	8		
17	5	10		Sixth column on Plate 51*b*.
	8	18	319-1	
17	14	8		First column on Plate 52*b*.
	8	17		
18	5	5		Second column on Plate 52*b*.
	8	17		
18	14	2		Third column on Plate 52*b*.
	8	17		
19	4	19		Fourth column on Plate 52*b*.
	8	17		
19	13	16		First column on Plate 53*b*.
	7	8		
20	3	4		Second column on Plate 53*b*.

At this point in the original, instead of 20 in the year series, we find a diamond shaped symbol, represented by 0 in our tables, with one black dot over it. From this it would seem that when this codex was written the Maya method of counting years was by periods of 20 each, as in the case of the month days. Whether there is any reference here to the ahaues is uncertain. I am inclined to think with Dr. Förstemann that it was rather in consequence of the use of the vigesimal system in representing numbers. It would have been very inconvenient and cumbersome to represent high numbers by means of dots and lines; hence a more practicable method was devised. It is evident, from the picture inserted at this point in the series, that some important chronological event is indicated. Here also in the written characters over this picture is the symbol for 20. The last number given in the above addition may therefore, in order to correspond with the method of the codex, be written as follows:

Twenty year periods.	Years.	Months.	Days.
1	0	3	4

Continuing the addition in this way the result is as follows:

Twenty year periods.	Years.	Months.	Days.	
1	0	3	4	
		8	17	
1	0	12	1	Third column on Plate 53*b*.
		8	17	
1	1	2	18	Fourth column on Plate 53*b*.
		8	17	
1	1	11	15	Fifth column on Plate 53*b*.
		8	17	
1	2	2	12	First column on Plate 54*b*.
		8	17	

1	2	11	9			Second column on Plate 54b.
		8	17			
1	3	2	6			Third column on Plate 54b.
		7	8			
1	3	9	14			Fourth column on Plate 54b.
		8	17			
1	4	0	11			Fifth column on Plate 54b.
		8	17			
1	4	0	8			First column on Plate 55b.
		8	18	321-1		
1	5	0	6			Second column on Plate 55b.
		8	17			
1	5	9	3			Third column on Plate 55b.
		8	17			
1	6	0	0			Fourth column on Plate 55b.
		8	17			
1	6	8	17			Fifth column on Plate 55b.
		8	17			
1	6	17	14			Sixth column on Plate 55b.
		8	17			
1	7	8	11			Seventh column on Plate 55b.
		7	8			

	1		7			15			19		Eighth column on Plate 55*b*.
						8			17		
	1		8			6			16		First column on Plate 56*b*.
						8			18	321-2	
	1		8			15			14		Second column on Plate 56*b*.
						8			17		
	1		6			6			11		Third column on Plate 56*b*.
						8			17		
	1		9			15			8		Fourth column on Plate 56*b*.
						8			17		
	1		10			6			5		First column on Plate 57*b*.
						7			8		
	1		10			15			2		Second column on Plate 57*b*.
						7			8		
	1		11			4			10		Third column on Plate 57*b*.
						8			17		
	1		11			13			7		Fourth column on Plate 57*b*.
						8			17		
	1		12			13			1		Fifth column on Plate 57*b*.
						8			17		
	1		12			13			1		First column on Plate 58*b*.
						8			17		

	1			13			3			18		Second column on Plate 58*b*.

The proof, therefore, that the theory advanced in regard to the order and the plan of the series is correct seems to be conclusive. This probably would have been conceded without the repeated additions given, but these were deemed necessary because of several irregularities found in that portion running through Plates 53*a*-58*a*, which constitutes the first half of the series.

Turning back to our Table VIII, representing that part of the series on Plate 53*a*, we will consider the three lines of black numerals above the day columns, discussing the irregularities as we proceed.

The numbers in the first column are 7/17, or, according to the explanation given, 7 months and 17 days. There is apparently a mistake here, the correct numbers being 8 months and 17 days, as it is the usual custom of the codex to commence numeral series with the prevailing interval; moreover this correction, which has also been made by Dr. Förstemann, is necessary in order to connect rightly with what follows; the counters under this first column require this correction, as they are 8 months, 17 days. Making this change we proceed with the addition.

Years.			Months.			Days .			
			8			17		First column, Plate 53*a* (corrected).	
			8			17			
			17			14		Second column. Plate 53*a*.	

Here the author of the codex has made another mistake or varied from the plan of the series. As several similar variations or errors occur in this part of the series, it will be as well to discuss the point here as elsewhere. Dr. Förstemann, in discussing the series, takes it for granted that these variations are errors of the aboriginal scribe; he remarks that "It is seen here that the writer has corrected several of his mistakes by compensation. For instance, the two first differences should be 177 [8 months, 17 days] and 148 [7 months, 8 days], not 176 and 149," &c.

This is a strained hypothesis which I hesitate to adopt so long as any other solution of the difficulty can be found. It is more likely that the writer would have corrected his mistakes, if observed, than that he would compensate them by corresponding errors.

Going back to that part of the series in the lower divisions which has already been examined and commencing with Plate 51*b* (see Table VI), we observe that the numbers in the lowest of the three lines of black numerals, immediately over the day columns, and the first day of these columns are as follows (omitting the week days attached):

14   11   8   5   2   10

Ik. Cauac. Cib. Been. Oc. Ezanab.

Turning to the calendar (Table II) and using the Muluc column, we notice that the figures of this third line of black numerals denote respectively the month numbers of the days under them; that is to say, Ik is the fourteenth day of the month in Muluc years, Cauac the eleventh, Cib the eighth, Been the fifth, Oc the second, and Ezanab the tenth. This holds good through Plates 52*b* to 58*b* without a single exception, provided the diamond shaped symbol in the fourth column of Plate 55*b* is counted as 20. This test, therefore, presents fewer exceptions than are found in counting the intervals as before explained; yet, after all, this would necessarily result from the fact that the day Muluc was selected as the commencement of the series, and hence may have no signification in reference to or bearing on the question of the year series, especially as the years counted are evidently of 360 days.

Returning now to our Table VIII, representing Plate 53*a*, we observe that the number immediately over Kan in the first column is 17, whereas Kan is the sixteenth day of the month. Is it not possible that the intention was to designate as the ceremonial day Chicchan, standing immediately below, which is the seventeenth day of the month in Muluc years? Even though there is no reference to Muluc years, the intervals may be given upon the same idea, that of reaching, for some particular reason, the second or third day of the column instead of the first. This would account for the compensation of which Dr. Förstemann speaks, without implying any mistake on the part of the writer. These irregularities would then be intentional variations from the order of the series, yet so as not to break the general plan.

The interval between 6 Kan of the first column (with the month number corrected) and 1 Ymix of the second is 8 months and 17 days, as it should be; between 6 Muluc and 1 Cimi, 8 months and 17 days; and between 1 Cimi and 9 Akbal, 8 months and 17 days, thus conforming to the rule heretofore given, a fact which holds good as a general rule throughout that portion of the series in the upper division.

Continuing the addition as heretofore we note the variations.

Years.			Months.		Days.		Column.	Plate.
			17		14		Second.	53*a*.
			7		8			

1		7		3		Third.	53a.
		8		17			
1		15		19	323-1	Fourth.	53a.
		8		17			
2		6		16		Fifth.	53a.
		8		17			
2		15		13		Sixth.	53a.
		8		18	323-2		
3		6		11		First.	54a.
		8		17			
3		15		8		Second.	54a.
		8		17			
4		6		5		Third.	54a.
		8		17			
4		15		2	324-1	Fourth.	54a.
		8		17			
5		5		19		Fifth.	54a.
		8		17			
5		14	324-2	16		Sixth.	54a.
		7		8			
6		4		4		Seventh.	54a.
		8		18	324-3		
6	324-4	13		2		First.	55a.
		8		17			
7		3		19	324-5	Second.	55a.
		8		17			
7		12		16		Third.	55a.
		8		17			
8		3		13		Fourth.	55a.
		8		17			

8		12		10		Fifth.	55a.	
		7		8				
9		1		18		First.	56a.	
		8		17				
9		10		15		Second.	56a.	
		8		17				
10		1		12		Third.	56a.	
		8		17				
10		10		9		Fourth.	56a.	
		8		17				
11		1		6		First.	57a.	
		8		17				
11		10		3		Second.	57a.	
		8		17				
12		1		0		Third.	57a.	
		7		8	325-1			
12		8		8		Fourth.	57a.	
		8		17				
12		17		5		First.	58a.	
		8		17				
13		8		2		Second.	58a.	
		8		18	325-2			
13		17		0		Third.	58a.	
		8		17				
14		7		17		Fourth.	58a.	
		8		17				
14		16		14		First.	51b.325-3	

We have in what has thus far been given a satisfactory explanation of the meaning and use of the lines of numerals and also of their relation to the day columns, but we still fall short of a complete interpretation, inasmuch as we are unable to give the series a definite location in the Maya calendar or in actual time. It is apparent, however, that the series cannot by any possible explanation be made to agree with the calendar system as usually accepted, as there is nothing in it indicating the four series of years or the year of 365 days. It may be safely assumed, I think, from what has been shown, that the year referred to in the series is one of 360 days, with probably a periodic addition of one day, but the reason of the addition is not yet apparent.

If the numbers in the lowest line of numerals over the day columns indicate the days of the month, and those of the middle line the respective months of the year, it is evident, as before stated, that Muluc is the first day of the year throughout, a conclusion irreconcilable with the Maya calendar as hitherto understood. It is probable, however, that the month and day numbers do not refer to particular months and days, but are used only as intervals of time counted from a certain day, which must in this case have been Muluc.

The sum of the series as shown by the numbers over the second column of Plate 58*b* is 33 years, 3 months, and 18 days. As this includes only the top day of this column (10 Cimi), we must add two days to complete the series, which ends with 12 Lamat. This makes the sum of the entire series 33 years, 4 months, or 11,960 days, precisely 46 cycles of 13 months, or 260 days each, the whole and also each cycle commencing with 13 Muluc and ending with 12 Lamat. It is also worthy of notice that in the right hand column of characters (hieroglyphics) over the inverted figure in Plate 58*b* two numbers, 13 and 12, are found attached to characters which appear to be abnormal forms of month symbols.

On Plates 63 and 64 are three series of ten day columns each and three lines of numerals over each series. These are as follows, so far as they can be made out, the numbers over the upper series being mostly obliterated. The 0 denotes the red, diamond shaped symbol which is here sometimes given in fanciful forms.

TABLE XX.—*Table showing series of day columns, with lines of numerals.*

UPPER DIVISION.									
Plate 63.						Plate 64.			
	4		3						0
	8		6				0		16
	0		0		0		0		0
III	Chicchan.	III	Chicchan.	III	Chicchan.	III	Chicchan.	III	Chicchan.
	Kan.		Kan.		Kan.		Kan.		Kan.
	Ix.		Ix.		Ix.		Ix.		Ix.
	Cimi.		Cimi.		Cimi.		Cimi.		Cimi.

XIII	Akbal.	XIII	Akbal.	XIII	Akbal.	XIII	Akbal.	XIII	Akbal.

Plate 64.

	0		0						
	12		8		3		3		
	0		0		0		0		0
III	Chicchan.	III	Chicchan.	III	Chicchan.	III	Chicchan.	III	Chicchan.
	Kan.		Kan.		Kan.		Kan.		Kan.
	Ix.		Ix.		Ix.		Ix.		Ix.
	Cimi.		Cimi.		Cimi.		Cimi.		Cimi.
XIII	Akbal.	XIII	Akbal.	XIII	Akbal.	XIII	Akbal.	XIII	Akbal.

MIDDLE DIVISION.

XIX	5		4		4		4		4
IV	1		14		9		5		0
IV	0		0		0		7		16
III	Chicchan.	III	Ix.	III	Akbal.	III	Eb.	III	Ymix.
	Kan.		Been.		Ik.		Chuen.		Ahau.
	Ix.		Akbal.		Eb.		Ymix.		Oc.
	Cimi.		Men.		Kan.		Been.		Ik.
XIII	Akbal.	XIII	Eb.	XIII	Ymix.	XIII	Oc.	XIII	Cauac.

	3		3		3		3		2
	14		9		5		0		14
	5		14		3		12		1
III	Oc.	III	Cauac.	III	Lamat.	III	Caban.	III	Cimi.
	Muluc.		Ezanab.		Manik.		Cib.		Chicchan.
	Cauac.		Lamat.		Caban.		Cimi.		Men.
	Chuen.		Ahau.		Muluc.		Ezanab.		Manik.
XIII	Lamat.	XIII	Caban.	XIII	Cimi.	XIII	Men.	XIII	Kan.

LOWER DIVISION.

	2		2		2		1		1
	9		4		0		13		9
	10		19		8		17		6
III	Men.	III	Kan.	III	Been.	III	Ik.	III	Chuen.
	Ix.		Akbal.		Eb.		Ymix.		Oc.
	Kan.		Been.		Ik.		Chuen.		Ahau.
	Cib.		Chicchan.		Ix.		Akbal.		Eb.
XIII	Been.	XIII	Ik.	XIII	Chuen.	XIII	Ahau.	XIII	Muluc.

	1		1						
	4		0		13		9		4
	15		4		13		2		11
III	Ahau.	III	Muluc.	III	Ezanab.	III	Manik.	III	Cib
	Cauac.		Lamat.		Caban.		Cimi.		Men.
	Muluc.		Ezanab.		Manik.		Cib.		Chicchan.
	Ymix.		Oc.		Cauac.		Lamat.		Caban.
XIII	Ezanab.	XIII	Manik.	XIII	Cib.	XIII	Chicchan.	XIII	Ix.

By examining carefully the lines and columns of the middle and lower divisions of the plates—those represented in Tables XXI and XXII—we ascertain that the two together form one series; but, contrary to the method which has prevailed in those examined, it is to be read from *right* to *left*, commencing with the right hand column of the lower and ending with the left hand column of the middle division.

As proof of this we have only to note the fact that the series of black numerals over the day columns ascends towards the left. Assuming the lowest of the three lines to be days, the middle one months, and the upper one years, the common difference is 4 months and 11 days. Numbering the ten columns of each of our tables from left to right as usual and adding successively the common difference, commencing with the tenth column of the lowest division, of which Cib is the first day, the result will be as follows:

Years.		Months.		Days.		
		4		11		Over tenth column, lower division.
		4		11		
		9		2		Over ninth column, lower division.
		4		11		
		13		13		Over eighth column, lower division.
		4		11		
1		0		4		Over seventh column, lower division.
		4		11		
1		4		15		Over sixth column, lower division.
		4		11		
1		9		6		Over fifth column, lower division.
		4		11		

1		13			17	Over fourth column, lower division.
		4			11	
2		0			8	Over third column, lower division.
		4			11	
3		4			19	Over second column, lower division.
		4			11	
2		9			10	Over first column, lower division.
		4			11	
2		14			1	Over tenth column, middle division.
		4			11	
3		0			12	Over ninth column, middle division.
		4			11	
3		5			3	Over eighth column, middle division.
		4			11	
3		9			14	Over seventh column, middle division.
		4			11	
3		14			5	Over sixth column, middle division.
		4			11	
4		0			16	Over fifth column, middle division.
		4			11	
4		5			7	Over fourth column, middle division.
		4			11	
4		9			18	Over third column, middle division.
		4			11	
4		14			9	Over second column, middle division.
		4			11	
5		1			0	Over first column, middle division.

The red numerals over the first column of the middle division, except the lowest diamond shaped one, are omitted, as they do not appear to belong to the series.

It must be borne in mind that the 4 months and 11 days form the common difference between the corresponding days of the columns counting from right to left; that is to say, counting 4 months and 11 days from the top day of any column will bring us to the first or top day of the next column to the left. The interval between the other corresponding days of the columns is also the same if the same week numbers are assigned them.

This question arises here, Does the difference include the time embraced in the entire column? That is to say, Is this interval of 4 months and 11 days (referring, for example, to the tenth and ninth columns of the lower division, our table) the sum of the intervals between 3 Cib and Men; Men and Chicchan; Chicchan and Caban; Caban and 13 Ix, and 13 Ix of the tenth column and 3 Manik of the ninth column? If not, the columns do not form a continuous series or must be taken in some other order.

Although Dr. Förstemann discovered the order in which the series as a whole was to be read, and also the common difference—given, as is his custom, in days—he failed to furnish further explanation of the group.

In answer to the question presented I call attention to the following facts:

Commencing again with the uppermost day, 3 Cib, of the tenth column, lowest division, and counting on the calendar to 13 Ix of the same year, the interval is found to be 10 months and 18 days, which is much more than the interval between 3 Cib and 3 Manik (first of the ninth column), and of course cannot be included in it.

Reversing the order in reading the columns, but counting forward on the calendar as usual, we find the interval between 13 Ix and 3 Cib to be 2 months and 2 days, and, what is another necessary condition, the intermediate days of the column are included in this period in the order in which they stand, if read upwards. The interval between 3 Cib, uppermost day of the tenth column, and 13 Chicchan, bottom day of the ninth column, is 2 months and 9 days. The sum of these two intervals is 4 months and 11 days, as it should be on the supposition that the entire columns follow one another in regular succession. This proves beyond question that the columns are to be read from *bottom* to *top* and that they follow one another from *right* to *left*. This enables us to fix the week numbers to the intermediate days and to determine the day to which the entire series is referred as its starting point. The days and their numbers of the tenth and ninth columns of the lower division, writing them in reverse order, that is, from bottom to top, are as follows: 13 Ix; 3 Caban; 11 Chicchan; 8 Men; 3 Cib; 13 Chicchan; 3 Lamat; 11 Cib; 8 Cimi; 3 Manik.

These numbers hold good throughout the series.

Commencing with 13 Ix, the lowest day of the tenth column, lower division, but first day of the series, and ending with 13 Akbal, the bottom of the first column, middle series, the time embraced is 5 years, 1 month, 0 day, less 4 months and 11 days—that is, 4 years, 14 months, 9 days (years of 360 days being understood). This is easily proved by counting on the calendar 4 years, 14 months, and 9 days from 13 Ix, as it brings us to 13 Akbal. If we add to this time 2 months and 2 days—the interval between 13 Akbal and 3 Chicchan (top day of first column, middle division)—we have, as the entire period embraced in the series as it stands—from 13 Ix (first of the series) to 3 Chicchan (the last)—4 years, 16 months, 11 days. Add to this 4 months and 11 days, in order to reach the day with which the count begins, and we have as the entire period 5 years, 3 months, 2 days = 5 years, 1 month, 0 day + 2 months, 2 days. If we count back 4 months and 11 days from 13 Ix (first of the series), we reach 1 Kan, the day to which the series is referred as its starting point. Counting forward from this date 5 years, 3 months and 2 days brings us to 3 Chicchan, the last day of the series.

It is worthy of notice that, although this series appears to be referred to Kan years, it is at variance with the idea of passing from one to the other of the four year series, and is, moreover, based upon the year of 360 days. The order in which it is to be read, which is true also of some other pages, indicates that these extracts pertain to a different original codex than those to which we have heretofore alluded, a conclusion reached by Dr. Förstemann soon after he commenced the study of the Dresden manuscript.

I was for a time inclined to believe there was a break between Plates 64 and 65, as there appeared to be no day columns with which the lines of numerals running through Plates 65-69 could be connected, but the fact that the sum of the black numbers in each is 91, precisely the interval between the corresponding days of the columns in Plates 63 and 64, will probably warrant the conclusion that they are connected with them. This conclusion is strengthened, so far as those in the lower division are concerned, by the fact that by taking the XIII attached to the lowest days of the columns the numbers properly succeed one another and the series conforms to the rule heretofore given. As proof of this I give here the lower line of the lower division, prefixing the XIII, thus: XIII; 9, IX; 5, I; 1, II; 10, XII; 6, V; 2, VII; 11, V; 7, XII; 3, II; 12, I; 8, IX; 4, XIII; 13, XIII.

Adding together the numbers and casting out the thirteens, thus, XIII + 9 - 13 = IX; IX + 5 - 13 = I, &c., the connection is seen to be regular. The final red numeral is XIII, the same as that with which the series begins, and the sum of the black numbers, 9, 5, 1, 10, 6, 2, 11, 7, 3, 12, 8, 4, 13, is 91, a multiple of 13. The middle line of numerals also connects with the XIII attached to the bottom symbols of the day columns; and the upper line of numerals connects with the III attached to the top symbols of the day columns.

Plates 70 to 73 present some peculiarities difficult to account for. That these pages belong to the same type as 62, 63, and 64 cannot be doubted, and that as a general rule they are to be read from right to left is easily proved; but this method does not seem to be adopted throughout, the order being apparently reversed in a single series.

The aboriginal artist has apparently made up these pages from two older manuscripts or changed and added to his original. The last two columns of Plate 70 and first five of 71 appear to have been thrust in here as an afterthought or as a fragment from some other source, forming apparently no legitimate connection with the series to either the right or to the left of them. It is true, as will be shown, that there is some connection with the lowest series on the right, but it would seem that advantage was here taken of accidental correspondence rather than that this correspondence was the result of a preconceived plan.

Commencing in the lower part of the middle division of Plate 73 and running back (to the left) to the sixth column of 71 and returning to the lower part of the lower division of 73 and ending with the sixth column of 71, is the following series. The columns are given in the order in which they stand on the respective plates, but the plates are taken in reverse order:

TABLE XXIII.—*Table giving comparison between Plates 71, 72, and 73.*

		First column.	Second column.	Third column.	Fourth column.	Fifth column.		
Plate 73, middle division	—	16	1	9	6	3	—	—
		5	0	15	10	5	—	—
		IV Caban.	IV Eb.	IV Manik.	IV Ik.	IV Caban.	—	—
		First column.	Second column.	Third column.	Fourth column.	Fifth column.	Sixth column.	Seventh column.
Plate 72, middle division	—	2	1	1	1	1	1	—
		3	17	14	11	8	4	19
		0	15	10	5	0	15	10
		IV Eb.	IV Manik.	IV Ik.	IV Caban.	IV Eb.	IV Manik.	IV Ik.
							Sixth column.	Seventh column.

Plate 71, middle division							
—	—	—	—	—	—	2	2
	—	—	—	—	—	9	6
	—	—	—	—	—	10	5
	—	—	—	—	—	IV Ik.	IV Caban.

	First column.	Second column.	Third column.	Fourth column.	Fifth column.		
Plate 73, lower division	3	3	3	2	2	—	—
	7	3	1	16	12	—	—
	15	10	5	0	15	—	—
	IV Manik.	IV Ik.	IV Caban.	IV Eb.	IV Manik.	—	—

	First column.	Second column.	Third column.	Fourth column.	Fifth column.	Sixth column.	Seventh column.
Plate 72, lower division	4	4	4	4	2	3	3
	12	9	6	2	17	14	11
	10	5	0	15	10	5	0
	IV Ik.	IV Caban.	IV Eb.	IV Manik.	IV Ik.	IV Caban.	IV Eb.

						Sixth column.	Seventh column.
Plate 71, lower division	—	—	—	—	—	5	4
	—	—	—	—	—	1	15
	—	—	—	—	—	0	15
	—	—	—	—	—	IV Eb.	IV Manik.

The interval between the successive days, counting to the left, is in each case 3 months and 5 days, corresponding with the numbers over IV Caban, fifth column, middle division, Plate 73. Commencing with this number and adding it successively, we obtain the numbers over the various columns:

Years.				Months.		Days.		
				3		5		Over fifth column, middle division, Plate 73.
				3		5		
				6		10		Over fourth column, middle division, Plate 73.

				3			5	
				9			15	Over third column, middle division, Plate 73.
				3			5	
				13			0	Over second column, middle division, Plate 73.
				3			5	
				16			5	Over first column, middle division, Plate 73.
				3			5	
1				1	333-1		10	Over seventh column, middle division, Plate 72.
				3			5	
1				4			15	Over sixth column, middle division, Plate 72.
				3			5	
1				8			0	Over fifth column, middle division, Plate 72.
				3			5	
1				11			5	Over fourth column, middle division, Plate 72.
				3			5	
1				14			10	Over third column, middle division, Plate 72.
				3			5	
1				17			15	Over second column, middle division, Plate 72.
				3			5	
2				3			0	Over first column, middle division, Plate 72.
				3			5	

2			6			5		Over seventh column, middle division, Plate 71.
			3			5		
2			9			10		Over sixth column, middle division, Plate 71.
			3			5		
2			12			15		Over fifth column, lower division, Plate 73.
			3			5		
2			16			0		Over fourth column, lower division, Plate 73.
			3			5		
3			1			5		Over third column, lower division, Plate 73.
			3			5		
3			4			10		Over second column, lower division, Plate 73.
			3			5		
3			7			15		Over first column, lower division, Plate 73.
			3			5		
3			11			0		Over seventh column, lower division, Plate 72.
			3			5		
3			14			5		Over sixth column, lower division, Plate 72.
			3			5		
3			17			10		Over fifth column, lower division, Plate 72.
			3			5		
4			2			15		Over fourth column, lower division, Plate 72.

		3		5		
4		6		0		Over third column, lower division, Plate 72.
		3		5		
4		9		5		Over second column, lower division, Plate 72.
		3		5		
4		12		10		Over first column, lower division, Plate 72.
		3		5		
4		15		15		Over seventh column, lower division, Plate 71.
		3		5		
5		1		0		Over sixth column, lower division, Plate 71.

It is worthy of notice that the sum of the series as expressed by the final numbers is precisely that of the series on the middle and lower divisions of Plates 63 and 64, heretofore given, and embraces seven complete cycles of 13 months, or 260 days each. Counting back three months and five days from 4 Caban (the day in the fifth column, middle division, of Plate 73) we reach 5 Been as the starting point of the series.

As there can be no doubt that the lines and days of the two divisions form together one unbroken series, it is evident there is no connection between that portion of it in the middle division and what lies to the left of it in Plate 71; but there does appear to be, as before indicated, some connection between the conclusion and what follows to the left in the lower portion of 71. The series which lies to the left at this point is as follows:

TABLE XXIV.—*Table showing relations of Plates 70 and 71.*

Plate 70.		Plate 71.					
5th column.	6th column.	1st column.	2d column.	3d column.	4th column.	5th column.	6th column.
6	5	4	3	2			
1	1	0	0	0	15	10	5
6	2	16	12	8	3	2	1
0	0	0	0	0	0	0	0

IV Eb.	IV Eb.	IV Eb.	IV Eb.	IV Eb.	IV Eb.	IV Eb.	IV Eb.

For the purpose of assisting the reader to see the relation more clearly, the last column of the preceding series—sixth of the lower division on Plate 71—is added at the right as it stands in the original.

It is apparent that the figures in the fifth column of 71 are exactly double those in the sixth column. This and the fact that the day IV Eb is the same as those following are the only indications that there is any connection between the series. Using the 5 years and 1 month as the common difference and adding, the result is as follows:

Years.	Months.	Days.	
5	1	0	Sixth column, lower division, Plate 71.
5	1	0	
10	2	0	Fifth column, lower division, Plate 71.
5	1	0	
15	3	0	Fourth column, lower division, Plate 71.

At this point another change occurs: the former difference is added to the last figures and the sum is doubled.

Twenty year periods.	Years.	Months.	Days.	
	15	3	0	
	5	1	0	
1	0	4	0	
			2	
2	0	8	0	Third column lower division, Plate 71.
1	0	4	0	
3	0	12	0	Second column, lower division, Plate 71.
1	0	4	0	
4	0	16	0	First column, lower division, Plate 71.

1		0		4		0	
5		1		2		0	Sixth column, lower division, Plate 70.
1		0		4		0	
6		1		6		0	Fifth column, lower division, Plate 70.

This series does not end at this point, but is continued in the lines immediately above, which are as follows:

TABLE XXV.—*Table showing relations between Plates 70 and 71.*

Plate 70.		Plate 71.					
5th column.	6th column.	1st column.	2d column.	3d column.	4th column.	5th column.	
1							
0	8(?)	15	13	10	9	7	
				XII			
12	1	3	2	2	2	1	
				II			
3	10	6	16	4	0	10	
				XII			
0	0	0	0	(?)	0	0	
IV Eb.	IV Eb.	IV Eb.	IV Eb.	IV Eb.	IV Eb.	IV Eb.	

Adding the difference, 1, 0, 4, 0, to the final result of the preceding addition we obtain the figures of the right hand column (fifth column, Plate 71) of this series:

6		1		6		0
1		0		4		0
7		1		10		0

To obtain the figures of the fourth column this difference must be doubled, thus

7		1		10		0
2		0		8		0

9		2		0		0

To obtain the black numbers of the next (third) column, the lower cipher symbol of which is wanting, we add the former difference:

9		2		0		0
1		0		4		0
10		2		4		0

This decrease in the difference is unusual and indicates some error. This idea seems to be confirmed in the following way: In order to obtain the numbers of the next (second) column it is necessary to add three times the former difference, thus:

10		2		4		0	
3		0		12		0	
13		2		16		0	Second column, Plate 71.

If the increased difference, 2, 0, 8, 0, were retained after its appearance the result would be as follows:

7		1		10		0	Fifth column, Plate 71.
2		0		8		0	
9		2		0		0	Fourth column, Plate 71.
2		0		8		0	
11		2		8		0	Third column, Plate 71.
2		0		8		0	
13		2		16		0	Second column, Plate 71.
2		0		8		0	
15		3		6		0	First column, Plate 71.

Adding the difference, 2, 0, 8, 0, to the third column, Plate 71, thus:

10		2		4		0
2		0		8		0
12		2		12		0

we obtain the red numerals inserted in the third column. It is probable that the original or some subsequent scribe, observing an error at this point, inserted these figures as a correction. If so, he failed to remedy the confusion apparent in this portion of the series. The sum of the entire series is 303 years (360 days each) and six months, equal to 420 cycles of 260 days.

I am strongly inclined to believe that this section and also pages 24 and 59 are interpolations by some aboriginal artist of a mathematical turn and advanced ability in this direction, who has given these high series more as curiosities than with reference to any specific dates or periods of time.

FIG. 371. Specimens of ornamental loops from page 72, Dresden Codex.

Commencing in the sixth column of Plate 71*a* and running through 72*a* to the second column of 73*a*, is a numeral series which presents some peculiarities that baffle all attempts at explanation. Contrary to the rule which prevails in these pages it ascends from left to right and has no day symbols connected with it. In addition to this, the numbers of its lowest line are inclosed in loops of the form here shown (Fig. 371) and have no apparent connection with the other lines of the series, but, on the contrary, if taken from right to left, they present in the order usually given the numbers of the ahaues or katunes.337-1 It is as follows:

						1	1	1	1	1	1	1	
2	5	8	10	13	16	0	3	6	9	11	14	17	
													II.
14	8	2	16	10	4	18	12	6	0	14	7(?)	2	XIV
⑪	⑬	②	④	⑥	⑧	⑩	⑫	①	③	⑤	⑦	⑨	

The last (thirteenth) column of this series is not in a line with the others, but is found in the lower part of the right hand column of Plate 73, and in connection with it we find the red numerals II and XIV, denoting the difference between the columns, as is apparent from the additions here given:

Years.			Months.			Days.		
			2			14		First or left hand column.
			2			14		
			5			8		Second column.
			2			14		

	8		2			Third column.
	2		14			
	10		16			Fourth column.
	2		14			
	13		10			Fifth column.
	2		14			
	16		4			Sixth column
	2		14			
1	0		18			Seventh column.
	2		14			
1	3		12			Eighth column.
	2		14			
1	6		6			Ninth column.
	2		14			
1	9		0			Tenth column.
	2		14			
1	11		14			Eleventh column.
	2		14			
1	14		8		338-1	Twelfth column.
	2		14			
1	17		2			Thirteenth column.

261-1 The work here referred to is entitled Die Mayahandschrift der Königlichen öffentlichen Bibliothek zu Dresden, herausgegeben von Prof. Dr. E. Förstemann, Hofrat und Oberbibliothekar. It contains, besides the chromolithographs of the 74 plates, an introduction published at Leipzig, 1880, 4º.

269-1 A Study of the Manuscript Troano, by Cyrus Thomas, pp. 7-15.

272-1 This method will be adopted throughout this paper where figures containing numerals are introduced.

273-1 In the representations of lines and columns of the codex Roman numbers are necessarily used to distinguish the class of numerals, yet in the text, as in this case, the Arabic numbers will be used as most convenient.

273-2 Strictly speaking, the interval between 11 Men and 13 Oc is fourteen days, but throughout this paper, by *"interval between"* two days, is to be understood the number of days to be counted *from* one *to and including* the other. The one counted from is always *excluded* and the one reached or with which the interval terminates is always *included.*

273-3 Science, p. 459, April 11, 1884.

277-1 Throughout this paper when the words "figure" and "character" are used in reference to what appears in the codex, they are to be understood as follows: "figure" refers to the picture, as of a person, animal, or other object in the spaces; "character" refers to the hieroglyphics or written symbols.

278-1 Study of the Manuscript Troano, by Cyrus Thomas, Chapters II and VII.

278-2 Erläuterungen zur Mayahandschrift, p. 2.

280-1 Erläuterungen zur Mayahandschrift, p. 16.

280-2 Bureau of Eth., Third Ann. Rep., pp. 16 et seq.

282-1 Study of the Manuscript Troano, by Cyrus Thomas, pp. 15, 16.

282-2 Déchiffrement des écritures calculiformes ou Mayas, par M. le Cte H. de Charency, Alençon, 1849; also, Mélanges, pp. 185-195.

283-1 For an explanation of the principle upon which these day columns were formed, see "Notes on certain Maya and Mexican manuscripts," by Cyrus Thomas, published in the Third Annual Report of the Bureau of Ethnology.

290-1 The symbol for this day in Kingsborough resembles Lamat, but the photographic copy makes it Ix, as it should be.

290-2 Förstemann, Erläuterungen zur Mayahandschrift, p. 42.

291-1 Erläuterungen zur Mayahandschrift, p. 36.

292-1 Erläuterungen zur Mayahandschrift, p. 60.

293-1 Erläuterungen zur Mayahandschrift, p. 56.

296-1 The bottom lines are selected because they are less injured in the codex than the top lines, which are in most cases entirely obliterated.

300-1 3 days in ms., should be 4.

317-1 The third symbol in the last day column of Plate 51*b* is Been in the codex; but this is an evident mistake, as shown by the order of the days, since Ahau, which has been substituted above, always follows Cauac. This may be seen by reference to the middle column of 57*b*.

319-1 This is one of the exceptional cases.

321-1 Second exception.

321-2 Third exception.

323-1 One line has been omitted in the numeral symbol.

323-2 Here we have again the added day.

324-1 The 8 at this point in the codex is an evident error.

324-2 Here is also an error in the original, this being 10.

324-3 The symbols require an additional day here.

324-4 The 8 in the year line in the original is a manifest error, as 6 precedes and 7 follows.

324-5 The 18 in the day line at this point is also an error, as the interval between 2 Muluc and 10 Cimi is 8 months and 17 days. Moreover, the next day number being 16 requires this to be 19.

325-1 The counters in the original at this point are certainly wrong, for here should be 7 months and 8 days, whereas the symbols are those for 8 months and 17 days.

325-2 Here we have again the additional day.

325-3 Added to show connection with the lower series.

333-1 Codex has 19, which is equivalent to 1 year and 1 month.

337-1 While reading the final proof I fortunately discovered what may prove to be the correct explanation of the numbers in the loops.

At the commencement of the series on Plate 71 and at its close on Plate 73 we observe the symbol of the day, 9 Ix. Starting from this date and counting forward on the calendar two months and fourteen days, we reach 11 Lamat. This gives the number in the first loop of the series. Two months and fourteen days more bring us to 13 Ik, the number in the second loop; two months and fourteen days to 2 Cib, the number in the third loop, and so on to the end. It is therefore probable that the numerals in the loops indicate the week numbers of the days, though these are usually expressed in red symbols.

338-1 The 7 in the twelfth column is an error; it should be 8, as an inspection shows the place of the missing dot. The additions make it clear that the numbers of the second line refer to months, those of the line below them to days, and those of the line above to years. The series is, therefore, apparently complete without the numbers inclosed in the loops.

CHAPTER II.

CONCLUSIONS.

The conclusions to be drawn from the foregoing discussion may be briefly stated as follows:

First. That the codex in its present form is composite, being made up from two or more different original manuscripts, as Dr. Förstemann has suggested.

Second. That a number of minor changes and additions have been made by a subsequent hand, possibly after it had assumed its present form.

Third. That the year referred to in the larger series is one of 360 days; also, that in instances of this kind the count is continuous, and hence not consistent with the generally received idea of the Maya calendar, in which, the four year series forms a necessary part of the system, unless some other method of accounting for the five supplemental days can be discovered than that which has hitherto been accepted.

Fourth. On the other hand, indications of the four year series are certainly found in all of the Maya manuscripts; for example, in Plates 25-28 of the Dresden Codex and Plates XX-XXIII of the Manuscript Troano,339-1 which seem to be based on this series; in fact, the numbers attached to the days in the latter can be accounted for in no other way. Plates 3-6 of the Cortesian Codex are apparently based upon the same system. The numbers in the loops on Plates 71, 72, and 73, Dresden Codex, heretofore alluded to and represented in Fig. 371, apparently defy explanation on any supposition except that they refer to the numbers of the ahaues, which are based upon the four year series.339-2 The frequent occurrence in connection and in proper order of both the first and the terminal days of the year apparently refers to the same system. Many of the quadruple series no doubt relate to the four cardinal points and the four seasons; yet there are some which cannot be explained on this theory alone.

It is impossible, therefore, to exclude this system from consideration in studying the chronology of the codices, although there are a number of the numerical series of the Dresden manuscript which cannot be made to fit into it on any hypothesis so far suggested. The same thing is also found to be true in regard to some, in fact most, of the series found in the Mexican manuscripts. This confusion probably arises in part from the apparently well established fact that two methods of counting time prevailed among both Mexicans and Mayas: one, the solar year in ordinary use among the people, which may be termed the vulgar or common calendar; the other, the religious calendar used by the priests alone in arranging their feasts and ceremonies, in which the cycle of 260 days was taken as the basis. But this supposition will not suffice as an explanation of some of the long series of the Dresden Codex, in which the year of 360 days appears to have been taken as a unit of measure, unless we assume—as Förstemann seems to have done—that what have been taken as years are simply high units and counting the whole as so many days, refer the sum to the cycle of 260 days, which will in almost every case measure them evenly as a whole, or by its leading factor, 13. That the smaller series attached to day columns are all multiples of 13 and referable to the cycle of 260 days has been shown by Förstemann as well as in the preceding part of this paper. But it is worthy of note that the difficulty mentioned occurs only in reference to series found in that portion of the Dresden manuscript which Förstemann has designated Codex B (page 24 being considered as belonging thereto).

The red unit number symbol, with a circle of dots around it, seen occasionally in the Manuscript Troano, seems to have some connection with the four year series. Take, for example, the one in the lowest division of Plate VII.

The series commences in the lower right hand corner of Plate VIII, where the day column with which it is connected is found. The days of this column, reading downward, are as follows: Ahau, Eb, Kan, Cib, Lamat, and the number over them is I, but without any dots around it, while the terminal I of the series is inclosed in the circle of dots. What is the meaning of this marked distinction? It is evident that it is something which does not apply equally to all the days of the columns; yet, as it is the terminal number, it must relate to some one of them. If we examine the series carefully I think the reason for the distinction will be explained; Written out in full, it is as follows:

I.		
Ahau		
Eb	}	10, XI; 10, VIII; 10, V; 10, II; 12[?], ⊙.
Kan		
Cib		
Lamat		

The last black number is 10 in Brasseur's fac simile, but should be 12. Making this correction, the series is regular and of the usual form. The sum of the black numbers is 52, which is the interval between the days, and the number over the column is the same as the final red number.

If we turn now to the calendar (Table II) and select Ahau of the Kan column, and 1, the seventeenth number of the eighth figure column, and count 52 days, we reach 1 Eb, the second day of our column as given above; 52 days more bring us to 1 Kan, the first day of the first month in the calendar and third day of our column. If the theory of the four year series be correct, then 1 Kan of the Kan series must be the first day of the first year of an Indication or week of years. This fact was probably considered by the aboriginal artist of sufficient importance to give this day a mark of distinction. As it is not possible for any of the other days of the column to be thus distinguished, it is fair to presume this peculiar marking of the final number refers to Kan. Moreover, this distinction would not occur if any other than the Kan series were used.

In the upper division of Plate IX of the same manuscript is the following series:

XIII		
Men	}	
Manik		20, VII; 20 ⓧ; 1, II; 4, VI; 7, XIII.
Cauac		
Chuen		
Akbal		

In this, I, the second red number of the series, has the circle of dots around it. The number over the column is partially obliterated, but is readily restored, and should be XIII.

If we select, on our calendar, the Cauac column, or series, a reason for this distinction will appear. The sum of the black numbers is 53, which is also the interval between the days. As has heretofore been shown, the red numbers of the series refer to certain days selected by the priests, for special reasons unknown to us, which occur between the days of the column.

In this case the intermediate days are as follows:

Between 13 Manik and 13 Cauac: 7 Manik, 1 Manik, 2 Lamat, and 6 Eb.

Between 13 Cauac and 13 Chuen: 7 Cauac, 1 Cauac, 2 Ahau, and 6 Kan.

Here we find the explanation for which we are seeking, as in the interval between 13 Cauac and 13 Chuen is 1 Cauac, which, if the Cauac column of the calendar be selected, is the first day of the year 1 Cauac, the first year of an Indication. As this occurs only when a year commencing with Cauac is selected, we infer that the series is based upon the system with the four year series.

The best illustration of this peculiarity and the strongest evidence of its signification is probably found in the series contained in the middle division, Plate XI, same manuscript. This, when written out and the numbers properly arranged, is as follows:

①	①		
Oc	Ahau	}	
Cib	Cimi		1, II; 2, IV; 2, VI; 5, XI; 2, XIII; 4, IV; 9(?) ①.
Ik	Eb		
Lamat	Ezanab		
Ix	Kan		

The last black number of the series is 9, but should be 10 to render the series complete. Making this correction, the series is of the usual type; the sum of the black numerals is 26, the interval between the days of the columns is 26, and the final red numeral is the same as that over the columns.

As the circle of dots is around the final red number and also around each of those over the columns, the distinction indicated must refer to one or more days of each column.

As the last days only of the columns are year bearers, the mark of distinction probably applies to them. Selecting for the left hand column the Ix series of years and commencing with 1 Oc, the seventeenth day of the eighth month, we count 26 days. This brings us to 1 Cib, the third day of the tenth month, or tenth figure column of our calendar and second day of the first day column of the series; 26 days more to 1 Ik; 26 more to 1 Lamat, and 26 more to 1 Ix, the first day of the year 1 Ix, which, according to the four year series, will be the first year of an Indication. Selecting the Kan series for the second column and counting in the same way from 1 Ahau, the seventeenth day of the eighth month, or eighth figure column of the calendar, the last day is found to be 1 Kan, the first day of the year 1 Kan, which must also be the first year of an Indication.

Unit numerals marked in this manner are found in two or three places in the Cortesian Codex, but there is none in the Dresden Codex. The series with which they are connected in the former, except that in the middle division of Plate 24, are too much obliterated to be traced throughout. This, by making two slight and apparently authorized corrections, is as follows:

①		
Cimi	}	

Ezanab		11, XII(?); 11, X; 6, III; 8, XI; 7(?), V; 9, I.
Oc		
Ik		
Ix		

The first red numeral of the line is X in the original and the next to the last black number is 6. By changing the former to XII and the latter to 7 the sum of the series will be 52, which is the interval between the days of the column.

Using the Ix column in the calendar and commencing with 1 Cimi, counting as heretofore, the last day of the column of the series is found to be 1 Ix, the first day of the year 1 Ix and the first year of an Indication, according to the four year system.

A somewhat remarkable confirmation of the theory here advanced is presented in a series found in the middle division of Plate II of the Manuscript Troano.

The series, when written out with the substitutes heretofore used, is as follows:

①	①		
Manik	Ymix	}	
Men (?)	Been		9, X; 6, III; 11, I.
Chuen	Chicchan		
Akbal	Caban		
Men	Muluc		

In Brasseur's fac simile the second symbol of the left hand column is clearly that for Men. If this be accepted as correct, then no year bearer (Kan, Muluc, Ix, Cauac) would be found in either column and the theory we have advanced regarding the signification of the dots around the red unit over the column would fall to the ground. Nor is this the only difficulty we meet with in attempting to apply the theory to this series. The sum of the black numbers is 26, which should also be the interval between the days of the columns. Counting 26 days from 1 Manik brings us to 1 Been instead of 1 Men; 26 more to 1 Cauac, a day not found in either column as given in the original. Taking the second column and counting 26 days from 1 Ymix, we reach 1 Manik, instead of 1 Been. This gives us the key to the series and solves the riddle. We must commence with 1 Ymix, then take 1 Manik, then 1 Been, and so on, going alternately from column to column.

Adopting this method and using the Cauac column of our calendar, Table II, the result is as follows: Commencing with 1 Ymix, the third day of the tenth figure column, and counting 26 days, we reach 1 Manik; 26 days more bring us to 1 Been, and 26 more to 1 Cauac, the first day of the first year of an Indication. The 1 Men of the left hand column should therefore be 1 Cauac, which is also proved by counting the intervals, without regard to the week numbers. For example, from Ymix to Been is 12 days, from Been to Chicchan 12 days, from Manik to Cauac 12 days, and so on through each column. Or, if we take the columns alternately, the interval is six days, thus: From Ymix to Manik, 6 days; from Manik to Been, 6 days; from Been to Cauac, 6 days; from Cauac to Chuen, 6 days, and so on to the end.

Although the proof is not absolutely conclusive that these red unit numerals have this mark of distinction for the reason given, it nevertheless furnishes what would seem to be a satisfactory explanation, and, if so, affords proof that the calendar system, based upon the four year series, was in vogue when the Manuscript Troano and the Codex Cortesianus were written.

This mark of distinction is found in a strange and unusual relation in the lower division of Plate XV, Manuscript Troano. The first red numeral of the series is given thus:

FIG. 372. Numeral character from the lower division of Plate XV, Manuscript Troano.

Most of the day and about half of the numeral symbols are obliterated, but all that are necessary for present purposes remain distinct and uninjured, as follows:

III,	}	
Ix		10, XIⓄI.
Cimi		

Judging by these and the few numbers remaining, the entire series was as follows:

III,	—	
Ix		
Cimi		10, XIII; 4, IV; 20, XI; 9, VII; 9, III
Ezanab		

Oc		
Ik		

The only doubt in reference to the restoration is whether the second and third pairs of numerals should be as given, or 2, II, and 22, XI. If we select the Kan column of our Table II and count from 3 Ix of the eleventh figure column, we reach 13 Kan. If the four year series was the system used 13 Kan might be the first day of a year, but not the first day of an Indication. As this is the only day referred to by the XIII which could have been the first of a year we must seek an explanation in something else. Counting ten days from 3 Ezanab will bring us to 13 Lamat, which is the last day (counting the five added days) of an Indication, commencing with the year 1 Kan and ending with the year 13 Kan.

According to my theory of the ahaues,[344-1] the year 13 Kan would have corresponded with the Gregorian years 1376, 1438, 1480, and 1532. According to the theory advanced by Perez,[344-2] it would have corresponded with 1385, 1437, 1489, and 1541.

It is therefore possible that this mark of distinction may be of some value in determining the relation of the Maya to the Gregorian calendar.

339-1 See Study of the Manuscript Troano, by Cyrus Thomas.

339-2 See note on page 337.

344-1 See Table XVII, Study of the Manuscript Troano, by Cyrus Thomas, p. 44.

344-2 See Table XVIII, ibid., p. 45.

CHAPTER III

THE WRITING.

It must be admitted that none of the attempts made at deciphering the writing in these manuscripts has proved entirely satisfactory; in fact there is still some doubt as to whether any of the characters are truly phonetic; nevertheless it is believed that what is here shown will tend to lessen this doubt. It must be conceded, however, notwithstanding these drawbacks and difficulties, that some material progress has been made towards a better understanding of its type and of the nature of the characters.

The direction in which it is to be read must of course be determined before any progress can be made in deciphering it. This was, until recently, a matter of speculation, but now may be considered settled. As this has been explained345-1 it is unnecessary to repeat that explanation here.

A certain parallelism in the sentences or groups of characters has also been discovered. Attention was first called to this by me in the work referred to, but is more fully explained by Dr. P. Schellhas in his paper entitled "Die Mayahandschrift der königlichen Bibliothek zu Dresden." It will readily be understood from a single illustration. Take for example the lower division of Plate XV of the Manuscript Troano (see Study Ms. Troano). Omitting from consideration the numerals and the day column at the left, there are here two short columns on the left and two on the right over the animal figures, and three longer columns between. As explained in the work referred to, the short columns are to be read as lines from left to right and the longer columns separately, from the top downward. There are, in all, five groups or sentences, each containing four compound characters. Representing these by letters, repeating those which indicate similar characters, and arranging as in the plate, the result is as follows:

b	*a*	*h*	*l*	*m*	*w*	*a*
r	*n*	*a*	*a*	*a*	*r*	*s*
		r	*r*	*r*		
		p	*k*	*t*		

In this case the characters represented by *a* and *r* are repeated in each group and in the same relation to the other characters. It is apparent, therefore, that each group is to be read separately, and, as each repeats in part what is given in the others, it is more than probable that they are simply short formulas to be repeated in certain religious ceremonies. This parallelism, though not always so apparent as in the case presented, is nevertheless found running through all the codices. The advantage to the attempts at decipherment which results from this fact is evident, as it will often justify the restoration of blurred or obliterated characters, and, what is of still more importance, will enable the investigator to test his conclusions by comparing the different characters and pictures with which they are associated.

Although it appears to be well settled that, as a rule, the writing, when in lines, is to be read from left to right—the lines following each other downward and the columns to be read from the top downward, but the groups, as before explained, to be read separately—it does not follow that the *groups* succeed one another from left to right. This has generally been taken for granted, but there are some reasons to doubt the correctness of this conclusion as regards a number of plates and possibly one entire codex.

The facts that the lines of numerals attached to the day columns extend to the right and that the written characters, when in lines, follow one another in the same direction lead us to infer that the groups and pictures follow one another in the same order, but the apparent movement of the latter towards the left would seem to indicate that *they* follow one another in *this* direction. This inference appears to be confirmed by the following evidence: As is well known, the plates of the Manuscript Troano are to be taken in reverse order to the paging. Turning to Plate II, we observe in the middle department of the middle division a bound captive or victim, on whose neck a machete is descending to sever the head from the trunk. Turning to Plate III, which properly stands to the left of Plate II, we see a headless trunk covered with blood and the fatal machete near the neck. It is fair to presume that this is the same individual that is figured in the preceding plate, and, if so, that the pictures follow one another toward the left.

Placing Plates XV* and XVI* of the same manuscript in the proper relation to each other and carefully examining the figures in the second division, we notice that the idol heads which the artisans are carving approach completion as we move toward the left, those in Plate XV* and the right hand one in XVI* being simply blocked out, while the middle one in the latter plate is completely rounded and is receiving the second ornamental line and the one at the left hand is receiving the third and final line.

The female figures in the second division of Plate XIX* indicate the same order, as shown by the increasing girth as we proceed toward the left.

The same order appears to be indicated in numerous places by the symbols of the cardinal points inserted in the text, as they (supposing the conclusion as to their assignment in my "Notes on certain Maya and Mexican manuscripts," accepted by Drs. Förstemann and Schellhas, to be correct) follow one another in the proper order if read towards the left, to wit, south, east, north, west.

As the writing over each figure, consisting usually of four compound characters, appears to refer to that over which it is placed, it follows that these character groups must be taken in the same order as the pictures. The suggestions on this point are presented here more as proper subjects of investigation by students of American paleography than as fixed conclusions of the writer. If found to be justified by the facts, they will furnish some additional aid in the work of deciphering these manuscripts.

SIGNIFICATION OF THE CHARACTERS.

As Landa's alphabet has so far proved useless as an aid in deciphering these manuscripts, our only hope of accomplishing this end is by long and careful study of these records and laborious comparisons of characters and the relations in which they stand to one another and to the figures.

Some discoveries made while preparing this paper for the press, which are mentioned further on, may possibly give us the key to the method used by Landa in forming his alphabet, and, if so, will probably furnish some slight additional aid in our investigations.

The direction in which the writing is to be read having been ascertained, our next step is to determine by comparison the probable signification of as many characters as possible before discussing the question of phoneticism. The relation of the characters to the pictorial representations forms our chief reliance in this branch of the investigation.

As a commencement in this work and as a basis for further attempts in the same direction, attention is now called to some characters, other than the day and month symbols, whose signification seems to be satisfactorily determined. As there is still some difference of opinion as to the assignment of the symbols of the cardinal points they are also omitted from the list. M. Léon de Rosny has given, as a supplement to his edition of the Cortesian Codex, a list of characters with their supposed signification. It is not my intention to discuss here the merits of this vocabulary, although I shall avail myself of so much found therein as appears to warrant acceptance.

The question of phoneticism will not be considered in connection with the list, as the subject will be briefly discussed at the close, the only object in view in giving the list being to indicate the signification of the characters alluded to. The Maya names appended are therefore to be understood simply as the supposed names applied to them or the objects they denote.

No. 1

Kal. The symbol for the number 20. Found in all of the codices and explained in the preceding portion of this paper.

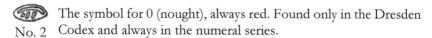

No. 2

The symbol for 0 (nought), always red. Found only in the Dresden Codex and always in the numeral series.

No. 3

Kin. Sun, and probably day also. It is not known positively that it has this signification except in connection with the equatorial cardinal point symbols and the symbol of the month *Yaxkin;* yet it is reasonable to suppose it has.

a

b

c

Aac or *Ac.* A turtle. That this symbol as shown in *a* and *b* denotes the turtle is conclusively proved by its resemblance to the head of that animal, as figured in the Cortesian Codex (see Fig. 373) and its relation to these figures. Found only in this codex, unless two doubtful symbols on Plate XXV*, Manuscript Troano, are to be considered as variants.

d

No. 4

FIG. 373. Turtle from the Cortesian Codex.

There can be no doubt that Landa's *A*, an exact copy of which is given in the margin, in both varieties, *c* and *d*, is nothing more nor less than this symbol; for, in addition to the very close general resemblance, we see in it the eye and the dot indicating the nostril. This fact is important, as it gives us some clew to the method adopted by Landa in forming his alphabet.

No. 5

Uech. Symbol or head of the armadillo of Yucatan. Appears but once or twice and in the Manuscript Troano only. (See Study of the Manuscript Troano, by Cyrus Thomas, pp. 98 and 145).

 *Che.* Wood. (See Study of the Manuscript Troano, by Cyrus Thomas, p. 144).

No. 6

 Cab. Earth, soil; also honey. (See Study of the Manuscript Troano, by Cyrus Thomas, p. 150.)

No. 7

 Piz. Stone or stone heap. (See Study of the Manuscript Troano, by Cyrus Thomas, p. 144). The Maya name of the thing indicated is uncertain, though I am inclined to believe *Piz,* as given in the work alluded to, is correct.

No. 8

 U. The left symbol of this figure appears to stand for vase, and is also used to indicate a pronoun or article when joined to another symbol, as here shown. (See op. cit., p. 145.)

No. 9

 Xicim. The ear. Rosny, Vocabulaire hiératique, No. 185.

No. 10

 Hau. The quarter of a deer. Usually represented as an offering to the gods; in all the manuscripts.

No. 11

 *Ikilcab.* The bee. Although the figure bears a much stronger resemblance to a beetle than to a bee, there can be no longer any doubt that Brasseur's supposition that it represents a bee is correct.

No. 12

Honey in the comb. (See Study of the Manuscript Troano, by Cyrus Thomas, Fig. 20); in the Manuscript Troano only, and always in red.

No. 13

Xamach or Chimix. A vessel. This symbol, found in all the codices, is apparently explained by its use in the upper division of Plate 27, Cortesian Codex, where it stands over each of four vessels or jars of the form represented in Fig. 374.

No. 14

FIG. 374. Jar from the Cortesian Codex.

This conclusion is greatly strengthened by the fact that the only other symbols in this connection are those of the cardinal points, one to each vessel. These figures are probably intended to denote here the four sacred vessels or amphoræ of the Bacab, though not surmounted, as Brasseur supposed, by human or animal figures.

The symbol appears to be used also in the ordinary sense, or at least to signify other vessels than the sacred four, if we may judge by its frequent repetition in Plate XIV, Manuscript Troano. But it is worthy of notice that here also, in both the middle and lower divisions, four of the symbols are connected with the cardinal point symbols; there is also in the former the figure of a vessel.

If this identification be correct it is important, as it has a strong bearing on the question of phoneticism. It will be observed that, although the right hand member resembles closely the symbol of the day Ymix, there are some differences, as may be seen by comparison. In the former the little figure at the top is divided as in Kan, and on each side of it there is a large dot, usually, and apparently by intention, circular or hollow. These differences are permanent in the different codices.

In the upper division of Plates X and XI, Manuscript Troano, where this symbol appears in connection with each of the four cardinal symbols, that

relating to the east presents this remarkable variation:

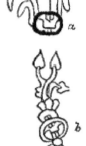

(?) A conventional figure of sprouting maize, never inserted in the text, but frequently in the Manuscript Troano and in the Peresian Codex made a part of the head gear of figures of deities, in which case the Kan symbol is generally omitted.

No. 15

The Kan symbol in this connection cannot be intended, as Dr. Schellhas supposes, to indicate the field or milpa in which the corn is growing, but the grain from which the plant is springing. (On this subject see Study of the Manuscript Troano, by Cyrus Thomas, pp. 105 and 107.)

(?) Symbol of a worm which gnawed the roots of the growing agave or maguey; appears but once, on Plate XXIX*c* of the Manuscript Troano.

No. 16

The animal head and teeth show the erroneous idea the natives had of the gnawing apparatus of insects. The worm is shown on the next page in Fig. 375.

FIG. 375. Worm and plant from Manuscript Troano.

FIG. 376. Figure of a woman from the Dresden Codex.

No. 17

Chuplal. Woman or female. This symbol is found in the Dresden and Troano Codices, but most frequently in the former. The appendage at the right is sometimes wanting, and occasionally that at the left, but when this is the case some other prefix is generally substituted.

If we examine carefully Plates 16-20 of the Dresden Codex, where this symbol is most frequently repeated, and compare it with the heads of the females there figured, it soon becomes apparent that the scrolls with the heavy black dot are intended to denote the locks of hair and that the symbol as a whole is, as usual, a modified or conventional form of the head (see Fig. 376).

No. 18

Otoch. A house or dwelling, or *Tabay;* a hut or hunting lodge. The symbol marked *a* is found in the Cortesian Codex on Plate 29; that marked *b*, on Plates 29, 32, and 34, same codex, and on Plates XVI* and XXII* of the Manuscript Troano. The one marked *c* is the usual form in the latter, as on Plates V*, VII*, and X*. It is also on Plate 38 of the Dresden Codex.

The relation of these symbols to the conventional figures of houses or huts inserted at the points where they are found, together with the form, which shows an attempt to represent the thatched or leaf covered roof, leaves no doubt that they are used for the purpose indicated.

No. 19

Buk (?). There are good and, it is believed, satisfactory reasons for concluding that these symbols are intended to denote the action of whirling a stick to produce fire or rolling a pestle in grinding paint. The first, marked *a*, is found only on Plate XIX of the Manuscript Troano, and the second, on Plates 5 and 6 of the Dresden Codex.

A copy of part of Plate XIX of the Manuscript Troano is introduced here (see Fig. 377) to show the relation of the figures to the characters. If this interpretation be correct, we see here an evident attempt on the part of the aboriginal artist to indicate by the symbol the action nec essary in the work to be performed. It is probably a conventional sign, and not a phonetic character.

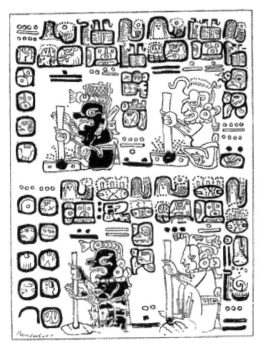

FIG. 377.

No. 20

(?) In all probability one of the symbols used to denote the act of walking or taking steps. Found but seldom in this particular form, though each portion occurs frequently alone or in other combinations.

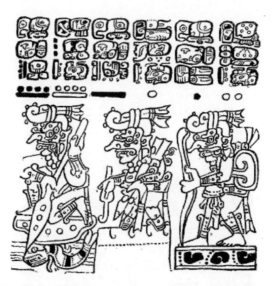

FIG. 378. Copy of lower division of Plate 65, Dresden Codex.

A remarkable series of figures and written characters runs through the lower division of Plates 65 to 69 of the Dresden Codex, apparently devoted entirely to the representation of incidents in the life of the culture hero Kukulcan, or deity mentioned on a subsequent page as the "long nosed god" or "god with the snake-like tongue," or to ceremonies to be performed in honor of this deity. Over the figure are three lines of written characters, as shown in Fig. 378, which is a copy of the lower division of Plate 65. These, as is readily seen, are in groups, one group of six compound characters over each figure of the god. There are thirteen figures of the god and thirteen of these groups of characters in the series. The characters of a group, as may be seen by reference to the figure, are arranged in the following manner:

a	*b*
c	*d*
e	*f*

to be read (presumably) in the alphabetic order of the letters given; though the order in which they are to be read is not essential at present. Examining the series carefully we find that the first character of each group corresponding with *a* in the above diagram is the same throughout. The same thing is true in reference to the third, or that occupying the place of *c* in the diagram, which is the symbol of the deity. The sixth, or that corresponding with *f* in the diagram, is also the same throughout the series; the fifth, corresponding with *e*, is substantially the same throughout, though subject to more variations than any of the other characters. It follows, therefore, that

- 112 -

the chief and almost the only differences in the readings of the groups are to be found in the second and fourth characters, or those represented by *b* and *d* in the above diagram; the others (at least those represented by *a*, *c*, and *f*), if referring at all to the figures, must relate to something found in or applicable to each. The third (*c*), as stated, is the symbol of the deity and corresponds in the text with the figure of the god in the pictures. As this deity figure is the only thing found in all of the representations, we must seek for the explanation of the other two permanent characters in something else than what is figured.

Comparing the second character (*b*) of each group with that upon which the god is seated or standing, we find sufficient evidence to satisfy us that this symbol is the one which is used throughout to indicate this object. For example, the second symbol in the group on Plate 69 is an exact copy of the object on which the deity is seated. The same thing is substantially true of that in the left hand group of Plate 66, the middle group of 67, and the right hand group of 68.

Assuming, on account of the remarkable regularity of this series and the fact that the deity is in each case seated or standing on something, that this rule holds good throughout, we have a clew to those corresponding symbols which are not simple copies of the things they are used to indicate.

Turning to Fig. 378, we observe in the right hand department the marks of footsteps under the deity and the character shown in the margin (No. 20) as the second of the group above the deity. It is worthy of notice that in the two we find precisely Landa's two characters for the letter B. Is it possible that the two principal parts of this compound character denote the Maya words *oc be*, "foot journey" or "enters upon the journey"? Attention will be called to this further on, but it is proper to state here that as the prefix is found in three other corresponding characters it cannot be a necessary part of that which represents the footsteps in this case.

No. 21.

Assuming the theory above given as to the characters in the inscription which represent the things under the deity figures to be correct, the second character in the middle group of the lower division of Plate 65, shown in Fig. 378, will be the symbol for the substance represented by scrolls under the figure of the deity.354-1

The prefix in this case is the same as that to the symbol above described (No. 20), and of course has the same signification. The other portion of No. 21 must therefore represent the substance in which the god is walking. This appears to be dust, sand, or mud.

No. 22.

Cacauak or *cacauche*. The wild or cultivated cacao. Found a number of times in the Dresden Codex, sometimes as represented in the marginal figure *a* and sometimes as in *c*, and always in connection with figures holding in the hand a fruit of some kind. It appears once in the Cortesian Codex (Plate 36), as shown in *b*, in connection with a fruit of precisely the same kind as that figured in the Dresden Codex. It is found also on Plate XVIII* of the Manuscript Troano, but is apparently used here to denote an action.

There can be little, if any, doubt, judging by the figures in connection with which it is found, that this symbol is used in the Dresden and the Cortesian Codices to denote the cacao. Whether it refers to the tree or to the fruit is uncertain; possibly the different forms in which it is found are intended to denote these distinctions. In some of the figures the capsule appears to be indicated; in others the seed. The prefix to figure *c* apparently indicates the heaping or piling up of the fruit on the dish held in the hands of the individuals figured in the same connection, as, for example, on Plates 12 and 13 of the Dresden Codex. If this supposition be correct it gives us a key to the signification of this prefix. Reference to its use in the upper division of Plate XVIII*, Manuscript Troano, will be made further on.

In this symbol we find another of Landa's letters, and, if phonetic, agreeing precisely with his interpretation.

No. 23.

Ekbalam according to Rosny. The variety marked *a* is found twice in the Manuscript Troano, Plates XVI and XVII, and that marked *b* once in the Dresden Codex, Plate 8, each time in connection with a spotted, leopard-like animal.

The black markings on the symbols render it probable that Rosny's interpretation is correct. The numeral before the first form may possibly be explained by the fact that this symbol is used once (Manuscript Troano, Plate XII) to indicate the day Ix.

No. 24.

Moo. The ara, a large species of parrot. This symbol is found but once, and that in Plate 16*c*, Dresden Codex, in connection with the bird shown in Fig. 379.

FIG. 379. The moo or ara from Plate 16. Dresden Codex.

The conclusion in this case is based on the following evidence: In this series there are six groups of characters, four compound characters in each group, arranged as in the annexed diagram:

a	b	e	d	g	h	i	m	o
c	d	c	f	c	d	c	n	b
1		2		3		k	c	c
						l	l	p

Similar characters in the different groups are represented by the same letter; for example, the symbol for woman, heretofore shown (No. 17), is represented by *c*, and an unknown character by *d*. Different letters represent different symbols. It is apparent that we have here the parallelism heretofore spoken of and are justified in basing conclusions on this fact.

At 1, 2, and 3 are female figures with a bird in each case perched on the back. At *a* is the head of a bird, evidently the symbol of the bird on the female below; at *i*, in the fourth group, is precisely the same symbol as the one found in the same relative position in the middle division of Plate 17 over another bird, and at *m*, in the fifth group, is another bird's head. From these facts we conclude that the first symbol in each of these groups denotes a bird, and, as no two are alike, that they refer to different species, the one at *g* corresponding with symbol No. 24, the bird beneath being the great parrot or ara. Other facts, derived from a careful study of the various groups of this portion of the codex, which would require much space and numerous illustrations to explain, lead to the same belief.

According to this conclusion, the following symbols also denote birds, probably of the species here indicated.

No. 25.

Icim? The horned owl. This is represented by *a* in the first group in the above diagram.

The bird in the figure under the group, although horned, bears but slight resemblance to an owl; yet, comparing the marks on the tail with those of two of the birds on Plate XVIII* of the Manuscript Troano, I think the interpretation is justified.

Kukuitz? The Quetzal. The symbol is apparently incomplete, but the bird figured under it justifies this conclusion. This symbol is represented by *e* in the above diagram.

No. 26.

If this interpretation be correct, we find in this symbol another of Landa's letters.

 a

 b

No. 27.

Kuch. A vulture or bird of prey much like the sopilote. These two symbols (*a* and *b*) appear to refer to the same bird, evidently a vulture. (See Manuscript Troano, Plates XVII*a* and XXVI*a*.) The first form (*a*) is found but once (Manuscript Troano, Plate XVII*a*), the other at several points, both in the Manuscript Troano and the Dresden Codex, and is represented by *m* in the preceding diagram.

If this determination be correct, the first of these symbols (*a*) is probably phonetic and agrees with the interpretation of No. 26.

No. 28.

Chom, Xchom, or *Hchom.* The sopilote or vulture. Found only in Plates 16 and 17, Dresden Codex. The bird figure in Plate 17 appears to be intended to represent a vulture. The symbol corresponds to *i* in the preceding diagram.

If phonetic, the word indicated should, according to Landa's alphabet, be aspirated, which is found to be true of one of the forms given by Perez.

In certain series of the Dresden Codex, which appear to relate to the four year series or to the four seasons, especially those on Plates 29-31, a certain class of food animals seems to be assigned to each. The four following symbols are those used to express this idea:

No. 29.

Ceh? The symbol for game quadrupeds. The same idea appears to be indicated by the folded and tied quarter of a deer, as shown in No. 11. The head shown in the symbol is probably intended for that of the deer, though more like that of the rabbit.

Cutz or *Cax*. The symbol for game birds, the head being probably that of the wild turkey (*Cutz* or *Ahcutz*).

No. 30.

Huh. The symbol for food reptiles or the iguana.

No. 31.

As the Kan figure is admitted to be a maize or bread symbol, it is readily seen that the object in view in connecting it with the animal figures is to indicate that they are used for food, and hence are proper offerings to the gods, which is equivalent to saying, to the priests.

Cay. The symbol for food fishes, or fishes in general, though as often on the Kan symbol or without any suffix.

No. 32.

Cutz or *Cax*. In one of the two series of these food symbols, in Plates 29-31 of the Dresden Codex, in place of the bird symbol No. 30 is that shown in symbol No. 33. It probably has, as Rosny supposes, the same signification, a supposition which is strengthened by the fact that it is found in the bird series on Plates 16*c* and 17*c*, same codex, and is represented by *o* in the preceding diagram.

No. 33.

SYMBOLS OF DEITIES.

Ekchuah. The symbol or hieroglyph of the deity named "Ekchuah" by the Mayas and considered the patron and protector of peddlers or traveling merchants (Fig. 380).

No. 34.

FIG. 380. The god Ekchuah, after the Troano and Cortesian Codices.

The signification of the name of this deity is "The Black Calabash." The form and the shading of the symbol render it more than probable that it is a conventional representation of a divided or halved black calabash or gourd, cut for the purpose of forming it into a cup or dipper, which, in this form, is considered a symbol of this deity.

The evidence upon which this determination is based is that the symbol constantly accompanies the red mouthed, black deity. It is found, with a single exception, only in the Manuscript Troano, and chiefly in Plates II to V, relating to the traveling merchants. The single exception alluded to is on Plate 15 of the Cortesian Codex; here the god bears upon his back the traveling pack, indicating the vocation of which he is the special guardian.

It occurs unconnected with the figure of the deity only on Plates IX*, XIV*, XV*, and XXV* of the Manuscript Troano. In the last the figure of the god is in the same division, but in the adjoining compartment. In Plate XV* it apparently refers to the idol the priest is carving, which is probably a black one intended to represent this god. Landa,358-1 speaking of the artists carving idols from wood, says:

They took also that which they used for scarifying their ears and drawing blood from them, and also the instruments which they needed for sculpturing their *black divinities*.

Its appearance in Plate XIV* is apparently in connection with the ceremonies relating to the manufacture of idols. Neither the symbol nor the god it represents is to be fond in the Dresden Codex.

a

b

c

No. 35.

Kukulcan. (?) This is the symbol of the long nosed god, which Dr. Schellhas designates "the god with the snake-like tongue," of which representations appear so frequently in the different codices (see Fig. 381).

The snake-like appendages hanging from the side of the mouth may possibly be intended to represent a curved fang rather than part of a divided tongue. A remarkable figure on Plate 72 of the Borgian Codex deserves special notice here. This is the representation of a deity supposed by Kingsborough and others to be Quetzalcoatl, in which the head is as represented in Fig. 382. Here we see both tongue and fang, and also an eye precisely of the form found in the Maya symbol.

FIG. 381. The long nosed god (Kukulcan) or "god with the snake-like tongue."

Whether Kukulcan is the god indicated is uncertain, unless he is identical with the long nosed god, or Maya Tlaloc, so frequently figured in the Manuscript Troano and the Cortesian Manuscript. It is only necessary to compare the figures on Plates 2 to 5 of the latter codex with the long nosed, green figures of Plates XXVI, XXVII, XXIX, XXX, and XXXI of the former to be convinced that they represent the same deity, and that this is the Maya Tlaloc or rain god, whatever may be the name by which he was known.

As the symbol which accompanies these is the same as that found in connection with the "snake tongued," long nosed god of the Dresden Codex, there is no doubt that the same deity is referred to. It is worthy of notice in this connection that Plates 29-41 of the Dresden Codex, which are devoted almost exclusively to this deity, refer very largely to water, the god being figured in connection with water no less than twenty-eight times. He is also twice colored black, probably to symbolize the dark rain cloud, and twice blue, denoting water. It is therefore fair to conclude that the author of this codex considered him the giver of rain.

FIG. 382. Copy of head from the Borgian Codex (Quetzalcoatl).

The following reasons given by Dr. Schellhas for supposing that the deity indicated is Kukulcan apparently justify his conclusion, though it is possible some other name may have been applied to him:

He is represented in all the manuscripts, and far more frequently than any other deity. His characteristic marks are always unmistakable. An entire section of the Dresden Codex, pp. 29-43, and pp. 1 and 2, belonging thereto, treat almost exclusively of this god, and wherever he is pictured there we also find his name hieroglyph. He is always characterized by the double, snake-like tongue hanging from his mouth and by the peculiar eye, two marks that are never absent, how numerous and varied soever may be his representations, his symbols, and attributes. We also find him with torches in his hands as symbols of fire; he sits on water; he stands or sits in water or in falling rain; he rides in a boat; he appears in company with a fish as symbol of water or in company of a bird's head as symbol of the atmosphere, upon the day sign *Cab* as symbol of the earth, sitting, with the ax (machete) in his hand, with arrows or spears, with a scepter, and finally, also, with the body of a snake. Considering the immense variety of this god's representations and the numerous symbols of power in the various elements which the deity rules, we may well be justified in assuming that there are indications here of one of the most important figures in Maya mythology, with one of the principal deities of the people. The most important god of the Mayas was Kukulcan, the creator of the country's civilization, who had come from the far, unknown east, the Mexican Quetzalcohuatl, the Gucumatz of the Kiche, the Kukulcan of the Tzendals. All these names mean "feathered snake," "bird snake." Now, in the above mentioned section of the Dresden manuscript, pp. 29-43, there is found on page 36, middle, the representation of a bird and a snake, the two symbols of the god Kukulcan, which, at the same time, denote his name in the manner of a rebus. That this representation is to be referred to the god with the snake's tongue is rendered probable on the one hand by the fact that this whole section treats of him and is proved on the other hand by the circumstance that in the same place the same snake is found represented with the head of the god; thus, page 35, middle, and 36, above. In the same way this snake with the god's head is also found in the Codex Cortesianus, page 10, middle, a passage which is rendered notable also by the fact that in the writing above the picture there is expressly found as a second sign the name hieroglyph of the god.

 Cimi (?). Supposed symbols of the god of death. Occurring very frequently in all the codices, but with several variations (see Figs. 383 and 384).

No. 36.

These are given chiefly on the authority of Drs. Förstemann and Schellhas, as I have some doubt in reference to this conclusion, for reasons which will here be given.

FIG. 383. The supposed god of
death, from the Dresden Codex.

FIG. 384. The supposed god of
death, from the Troano Codex.

As Dr. Schellhas remarks, this is "the most characteristic and most easily recognized deity of the Maya Codices"; but this statement will not apply to the symbols, as the variations are such as to render it exceedingly doubtful whether precisely the same idea is embodied in each. Even the two forms here given, both of which are found in all the codices and often together, present variations too marked for us to believe, except upon strong evidence, that they represent the same thing. Nor do the figures of this deity or supposed deity appear to embody throughout the same idea. In fact, they leave us in doubt as to whether any one recognized deity is to be understood. Was there in the Maya pantheon such a deity as the god of death? I have so far been unable to find any satisfactory reason for answering this question in the affirmative.

In the first part of the Dresden Codex, which is devoted, in part at least, if not chiefly, to the maladies of the country, the skeleton figures undoubtedly have reference to death, much like the skull and cross bones in our day. In other places, as Plates XXVII and XXII* of the Manuscript Troano and Plate 7 of the Cortesian Codex, the parched earth appears to be intended, but it must be conceded that here also the idea of death is included. Substantially the same idea, or at least the relation of this god to the earth, appears to be indicated in Plate 8 of the Cortesian Codex, where he is represented as beneath and holding up that upon which another deity, bearing the bread symbol, is seated.

As before stated the two symbols frequently appear in connection, sometimes where the god is figured and often where he is not. It is, therefore, unsafe to conclude as yet that either variety indicates a particular deity known as the god of death.

Symbol of the god with the banded face; seen chiefly in the Manuscript Troano; not found in the Dresden Codex (Fig. 385). This is not the deity which Dr. Schellhas designates as "the god with face crossed by lines."

No. 37.

FIG. 385. The god with the banded face, from the Codex Troano.

This deity evidently pertains to the underworld and is closely allied to the so-called god of death. The symbol and the figure are found together in but few instances, yet the peculiar markings are such as to leave no doubt on the mind, that the symbol is intended to denote what is represented by the figure, being simply the head of the deity as invariably figured. They appear together in Plates III*c*, V*a*, and V*b*, XXVIII**c*, and XXIX*c* of the Manuscript Troano, in the first two as having some relation to the traveling merchants, but in the last two in a very different rôle. The dotted lines with which the bodies of these figures are marked and the peculiar anklets appear to have been introduced to signify relationship to the god of death. Perhaps the most direct evidence of this relation is found in Plate 42 of the Cortesian Codex, where the two deities are brought together at the sacrifice here indicated. The two appear to be united in one in the lower division of Plate XXVI* of the Manuscript Troano.

Figures of this god are also found in some of the Mexican codices, as on Plate 73 of the Borgian manuscript, where the relation to death and to the underworld is too apparent to be mistaken. On Plate 10, same codex, the head of death is marked with the distinguishing black band.

Unfortunately for investigations in this line, the early Spanish notices of the Maya mythology are so brief and confused that we can derive but little aid from them in our efforts to identify the deities figured in these manuscripts. Possibly the one with the banded face may represent Cumahau or Hunhau, the prince of the lower regions; but the rôle he appears to play where figured, with the exception of Plate II, Manuscript Troano, and Plate 73 of the Borgian Codex, would scarcely justify the name.

(?) Symbol of the deity which Dr. Schellhas designates "the god with the old man's face." Found in all the codices and almost invariably in connection with the representation of the deity shown in our Fig. 386.

No. 38.

FIG. 386. The god with the old man's face.

The deity denoted by this symbol and by the figure which it accompanies is possibly Zamna or Ytzamna, a deified Maya hero, but the various rôles in which he is found make it difficult to decide on this point. He appears comparatively few times in the Dresden Codex, and only in the first few pages. In none of these is there anything to indicate his functions. In Plates 12c and 15c he holds a sun symbol in his hand, which might be supposed to refer to his attributes as "Kinich-Kakmo" but for the fact that the same thing is true of one or two other deities figured in the same codex. In the Manuscript Troano, where he is oftenest represented, his figure and his symbol appear most frequently in connection with the bee or honey industry; for example, on Plate Vc, the only place in the first part of the manuscript where honey appears to be referred to, and twenty-two times in that section of the second part, Plates I* to X*, relating to bees. He also appears to take an active part in the manufacture of idols, engages in painting, aids in the culture or gathering of cacao, engages in predatory excursions, and acts in various other relations. In the left compartment of Plate XXIV*a he bears on his head the head of a bird. In the remarkable double plate (41-42) of the Cortesian Codex he is twice figured, in the central area and at the east (top), and in each case is accompanied by a female deity. In the latter case both god and goddess are bearing in their hands the Kan or corn symbol. In Maya mythology Zamua was given a spouse named Ix Kan-Leox, which signifies the yellow frond or silk of maize.

Symbol, according to Dr. Schellhas, of the deity which he names "the god with face crossed by lines," found in all the codices, but most frequently in the Manuscript Troano and the Cortesian manuscript. The deity is usually represented as in Fig. 387.

FIG. 387. The god with face crossed by lines.

This is introduced here on the authority of Dr. Schellhas, although I have considerable doubt as to the correctness of his conclusion.

He remarks in regard to it as follows:

Another characteristic and easily recognized deity, which, it is true, is comparatively rare in the Dresden manuscript, but occurs with extraordinary frequency in other codices, and whose sign it is not hard to find, is the god whose face is crossed [surrounded] by peculiar parallel lines, representations of whom are given in the Cortesian Codex (p. 11, below) and Dresden Codex (p. 13, middle). The deity is always male and is found in the Dresden Codex five times, Cortesian Codex eighteen times, Manuscript Troano twenty times, and Codex Peresianus five times.

The sign of this god, as was the case with the others and as seems to be the general rule, consists merely of a representation of the god's head, combined with a sign which probably represents an affix. The sign is found wherever the deity is represented and is an exact rendering of the god's head, so that there can be no doubt as to its being the name hieroglyph. True variations are not found, the hieroglyph being perfectly alike in all the manuscripts.

The nature of this deity is not easily determined, though it occurs in the Codices Troano and Cortesianus with extraordinary frequency, so that it would be seen that these two manuscripts, which evidently belong together, treat principally of this deity. No analogous deity is found in Aztec picture writing. * * * To all appearances we have here a momentous figure of Maya mythology, of which, unfortunately, we know nothing.

It is true that this symbol is found in almost every instance where the figure of the god appears—in fact, with fewer exceptions than others in reference to which there is probably little doubt. It is also true that the symbol is an exact copy of the god's head; but on the other hand there are strong reasons for doubting the correctness of Dr. Schellhas's conclusion.

The first is that the figure of the supposed deity seems to have more indications of being the conventional representation of an idol than of a deity. The lines of the head are precisely the same as those on the heads of the carved idols.365-1

We also find it in connection with the wood symbol (marginal No. 6) at the only points where the latter is found in the Cortesian Codex, and, what is significant, in wholly inappropriate places unless connected with an idol figure. These are found in the lower division of Plates 10 and 11, two on the top of thatched roofs and another on the head of the deity called the "god with the old man's face," the head in the latter case being apparently carved from a block of wood.

The second is to the same effect, the symbol being found over each of the figures of the lower division of Plates 26, 27, and 28 of the Cortesian Codex and the middle division of Plates XXXI* and XXXII* of the Manuscript Troano, where there appear to be processions of the different deities. It is also significant that in the latter case each deity is bearing in his hands what seems to be a block of wood from which in all probability an idol is to be carved.

Third, we find rows or lines composed entirely of this symbol, as in the so-called title page of the Manuscript Troano.

DISCUSSION AS TO PHONETIC FEATURES OF THE CHARACTERS.

It must be admitted, as heretofore intimated, that this question has not as yet been satisfactorily answered. Whether what is here presented will suffice to settle this point in the minds of students of American paleography is doubtful; nevertheless, it is believed that it will bring us one step nearer the goal for which we are so earnestly striving. Something is said on this subject in my former work,365-2 which need not be repeated here.

As it is evident from the preceding list of characters that conventional signs and symbols, often nothing more than abbreviated pictographs, were used in many cases to designate objects and persons, the inference to be drawn, unless other evidence is adduced, is, that this method prevailed throughout. Nevertheless there is some evidence that at the date when these manuscripts were written Maya culture was in a transition state; that is to say, conventional symbols were passing into true ideographs366-1 and possibly into phonetic characters.

The lack of any satisfactory key to assist us in deciphering them makes it exceedingly difficult to decide how far this change had progressed. We are therefore left wholly to deductions to be drawn from the facts obtained by laborious comparisons of the various relations in which the characters are found and the uses which appear to be made of them in the manuscript.

It will be admitted without question that a large number of these characters are ideographs or conventional symbols, as distinguished from pictures, as, for example, most of those denoting the days, months, and cardinal points. I say most of these, as it is yet possible to learn from some of them the objects they were intended to represent, the characteristic features not being entirely lost, as the symbol for the day Cimi, the "death's head" or skull; that of the day Ymix, "the grain of maize;" that of the month Moan, "the head of the moo or ara," a species of parrot, &c.

It is also possible to show from the manuscripts themselves evidences of the changes from conventional pictographs to true or mnemonic symbols.

Take, for instance, the bird symbols on Plates 16, 17, and 18 of the Dresden Codex, presented in the preceding marginal figures numbered 24, 25, 26, 27, 28, and 33. If the determination be correct as given, it is apparent that, while one of the birds is indicated by the head as a symbol, the others are denoted by ideographs, or by phonetic characters bearing no resemblance to their forms or peculiar features. That numerous examples of this kind are to be found in these manuscripts will be admitted by all who have carefully studied them.

Another fact bearing upon this point is the difference between the Dresden Codex and the Manuscript Troano in regard to marking with symbols the things represented in the pictures. We fail to find in the former (unless that on Plate 30 be a possible exception) the earth or soil represented by any symbol, though frequently occurring in the latter and also occasionally in the Cortesian Codex. The symbol for wood or that appearing so often on wooden articles in the latter, and occasionally in the Cortesian Codex, is wanting in the Dresden Codex, though wooden articles are several times represented. From this we infer that the Manuscript Troano is a more recent production than the Dresden Codex, notwithstanding the evidences of greater skill in drawing and higher mathematical attainments shown in the latter.

Before discussing the question of phonography we ask attention to one or two facts regarding Landa's alphabet which do not appear to have been previously noticed, yet have an important hearing on the subject.

The failure to reach any satisfactory results with this alphabet proves, beyond a reasonable doubt, that this author was mistaken as to the character of the

Maya writing; yet the frequent occurrence in the manuscripts of most, if not all, of the elements he presents renders it certain that there is a basis of truth on which it rests. It is probable, therefore, if we can find the key to his method, we may, after all, obtain some satisfactory results by means of his alphabet.

I have already stated as my belief that—

He has undertaken to pick out of their compound or syllabic characters the letter elements; hence it is that, while we find it impossible to decipher the manuscripts by using them, yet we find such frequent resemblances as to compel us to admit a fundamental relationship.367-1

This opinion I still believe to be correct, but was, until very recently, unable to get any positive evidence as to his method of obtaining these elements.

While examining the Cortesian Codes I came across (on Plate 17) the symbol for a turtle (the different varieties of which are shown in marginal figure No. 4), which is nothing more or less than an attempt to represent the head of the animal. In the more abbreviated form (*b*) I at once recognized Landa's A (compare with *c* and *d*, No. 4). As the Maya name of the turtle is *Ac* or *Aac* it is apparent that in this instance the old Spanish priest selected a symbol representing an object the name of which contains a single syllable having, as its chief letter element, A. As this symbol is simply a representation of the animal's head there is no reason to infer that it is phonetic; on the contrary, it is more reasonable to assume that it was used only as a conventional sign. It is possible that after long usage it may have been adopted as a phonetic character, though its exceedingly rare occurrence in the manuscripts (being found only in the Cortesian Codex and with the turtle figure) and the fact that it is seldom, if ever, used as part of a compound character would seem to forbid this idea.

Precisely the same method was adopted in obtaining his B, which is given in two forms, first as a foot print and second as a circle inclosing four circular dots. The first, as all are aware, is only a conventional sign and presumably not phonetic. The second may be phonetic, though apparently but an abbreviation of the first. In Plate 65*c* (see marginal No. 20) and Plate 41*c* the two forms are brought into such relation to each other as to show that the latter is used as a symbol to represent the idea conveyed by the first. The proof in these cases is too strong to admit of doubt and explains Landa's method of obtaining his B, which, as before stated, was by selecting the symbol of that which is denoted by a Maya word of one syllable having B as its chief letter element, *Be* being the Maya word for "way," "journey," "walking," &c.

The symbol for the cacao given above in marginal No. 22 contains his eleventh letter *Ca* twice and is probably that from which it was taken; likewise that of the *Kukuitz* or Quetzal (marginal No. 26) and of the *Kuch* or vulture (marginal No. 27a), each of which contains his *Ku*, being double in the former and single in the latter. I am as yet unable to trace these two symbols to their origin; we might suppose, from Landa's figure of the latter, that it was intended to represent a bird's nest containing eggs, but an examination of the symbol as found in the manuscript renders this conclusion doubtful.

The evidences of phonography are few and, as must be admitted, not entirely satisfactory; yet they are apparently sufficient to justify the somewhat general belief that the writing of the Mayas had reached that stage where characters are sometimes used to indicate sounds. That comparatively little advance had been made in this direction at the time of the conquest is possible; moreover there is nothing to justify the belief that they made use of true letters as Landa supposed. If they had a phonographic system of any kind it was very imperfect and was only in that primary stage in which syllables are represented by single characters and words of more than one syllable by compound characters. Judging by the changes observed in the relation of the parts of compound characters to one another, we conclude that the order of arranging these parts was not uniform or essential. It is also doubtful, if any of these characters are phonetic, whether the parts of the longer words were always written out in full. I am led to believe, from a few slight indications, that, in forming words of more than one syllable, they often used only the leading phonetic elements of the single words of which they are composed; in other words, that they followed the rebus method of the Mexicans.

Descending to particulars and examples, the following are, perhaps, the strongest proofs which can be presented on this point:

As there can no longer be any doubt that the symbols for the cardinal points have been ascertained and that those relating to the polar points are distinguishable from those relating to the equatorial points, we are justified in referring to them in this discussion. As each of the two assigned to the equatorial points contains the symbol for "sun" or "day" and as the two Maya words for these points—*Likin* or *Lakin* and *Chikin*—contain the Maya term for sun or day ("kin"), there is some reason for believing that the characters are phonetic. There is to be added to this evidence the fact that the symbol of the month *Yaxkin* contains the same sun symbol. It would be somewhat remarkable to find the same single character in three different combinations, representing three different ideas expressed by words containing the same sound, yet having no reference to the sound.

It is now generally admitted by students of American paleography, on what appears to be satisfactory evidence, that symbol No. 7 of the preceding list,

Cab, is used to signify "earth" or "land" and "honey," both of which are designated by the same Maya term, *Cab*. As there is no similarity in the things denoted the character is probably phonetic. The "bee" appears also to be frequently indicated by the same character with an affix, as may be seen by reference to the lower divisions of Plates III*—X* of the Manuscript Troano.

The symbol No. 9 (U) of the preceding list is found repeatedly on vases and also as a prefix to both simple and compound characters. As *U* in Maya signifies "moon," "vase," and certain pronouns and is also used as a euphonic particle before vowels, we are perhaps justified in concluding that the symbol is phonetic and denotes the word *U*. I am aware that neither Perez nor Dr. Brinton gives "vase" as one of the meanings of this word, yet its constant appearance on vessels seems to leave no doubt that Brasseur is correct. Even admitting that he is mistaken and that we are in error as to the signification of the symbol, its various uses justify the belief that it is phonetic.

The symbol No. 34 of the preceding list, which is supposed to be that of the god Ekchuah, is probably phonetic. The name of this deity is composed of two Maya words, *ek*, "black," and *chu*, "calabash," and hence signifies "the black calabash," and the form and coloring of the symbol are apparently intended to denote this signification. If this interpretation be correct it is phonetic, as there is nothing in or pertaining to the figure of the deity which corresponds with it, except the color.

If the interpretation given of the preceding symbols Nos. 22, 24, 26, 27*a*, and 33 be correct, there can be scarcely a doubt that they are phonetic. In the first—*cacau, cacauak*, or *cacauche*, the "cacao"—we see Landa's letter *Ca*, which is doubled in each of the three forms taken from the different codices. In the twenty-sixth—*Kukuitz*, the Quetzal—Landa's *Ku* is duplicated, as it should be if phonetic, while in 27*a*, *Kuch*, it appears but once. There is here also an additional evidence of phoneticism in the fact that, while one of the symbols used to denote this bird shows simply its head, and is surely not phonetic, the other is entirely different and bears no resemblance whatever to any feature or characteristic of the bird. Moreover, both parts of it are used in other combinations referring to entirely different things.

If my interpretation of No. 14 (*Xamach* or *Chimix*) be right, it is probably phonetic also. It is composed, as will be seen by reference to the figure, of two symbols closely resembling that for the day Ymix, except that the top portion of one is omitted. The resemblance in sound to a duplication of Ymix is apparent. The slight but permanent variation of the right hand portion from the usual Ymix symbol and the omission of the top portion of the left hand one are scarcely explainable on the supposition that they form simply a conventional sign; but if phonetic the reason is apparent, as the *m* sound is not repeated in the Maya name. This conclusion is strengthened by the fact that the month *Mac*, found in the last or bottom line of Plate 49, is precisely the same as the right portion of No. 14, with Landa's symbol for *Ca* added. This probably justifies us in concluding that the true name of this month is *Camach*, "the jaw" or "jaws," and that Landa's figure is simply a rude representation of the lips or mouth.

I have expressed the opinion370-1 that the chief phonetic element of No. 8 (the stone symbol), if used to represent sound, is *p* or *pp*. This opinion seems to be confirmed by the fact that this character is found as a part of the symbol for the month *Pop* on Plate 50 of the Dresden Codex. (See the second character in the first transverse line below the day columns in the preceding Fig. 362.) The method of determining the months referred to in these plates of the codex has been given in the preceding part of this paper.

The interpretation given above of symbol No. 24 (the moo or ara) will probably be accepted by all students of these manuscripts, and if so its phonetic character must be conceded. That it is used in the place above alluded to (Dresden Codex, Plate 16*c*) to denote this bird is proved by the parallelism of the groups and the figure of the parrot under it. If we turn now to Plate 48 of this codex we observe that the second character of the first line below the day columns and the first character in the upper line of the lower group or square is, in each case, a bird's head. It is easily proved by means of the numeral series with which these are connected that they denote, in both cases, the month Moan (from the moo), proving that Brasseur's surmise was correct.370-2 If the same bird is represented by two symbols, one pictorial and the other having no resemblance to any feature or character of the thing denoted, it is probable the latter is phonetic. This conclusion is strengthened in this case by the strong resemblance of the first part of No. 24 to the symbol for the month Mol.

I have shown above that the right portion of No. 20 of the list is Landa's letter B, and also that in the lower division of Plate 65, Dresden Codex (see Fig. 378), it signifies "footsteps" or the act of walking. As the Maya word *Be* signifies "journey," "wood," "march," and also "journeying" and "marching," it is possible that this symbol is also phonetic, although apparently only a modified form of the footprint. This supposition is strongly supported by the fact that it is found in numerous and varied relations, single and in combination.

The symbol for 20 (*Kal*), No. 1 of the preceding list, is apparently phonetic. This view appears to be confirmed by its use otherwise than as a numeral symbol at several points in the text of the Manuscript Troano. For example, in the third division of Plate XVII* it appears in this form, ![glyph] while immediately below is the representation of an idol head in a vessel covered with a screen or basket, as shown in Fig. 388. The Maya verb *Kal* signifies to "imprison" or "inclose," which is certainly appropriate to what we see in the figure. As the symbol is over each of the three similar figures in the division, it is probable that it is intended to denote something relating to or observable in them. In the second division of Plates XV* and XVI*, same codex, is this symbol, ![glyph] several times repeated, and below each the figure of a priest or deity at work, each carving, with a machete or hatchet, the head of an idol. The probable signification is "Give twice twenty strokes with a machete," and hence is but partially phonetic.

FIG. 388. Wooden idol in vessel with basket cover.

Other examples bearing on this question may be found, but these are believed to be sufficient to warrant the belief that at the time these codices were written Maya culture had reached that stage where the idea of phoneticism was being introduced into the writing. Yet it is certain, and even susceptible of demonstration, that a large portion, perhaps the majority, of the characters are symbols. The more I study these characters the stronger becomes the conviction that they have grown out of a pictographic system similar to that common among the Indians of North America. The first step in advance appears to have been to indicate, by characters, the gesture signs.

345-1 See Chapter VI, Study of the Manuscript Troano, by Cyrus Thomas.

354-1 Unfortunately the scrolls were overlooked in preparing the cut.

358-1 Relacion de las cosas de Yucatan, p. 308.

365-1 See Plates XVI*b and XVII*c, Manuscript Troano.

365-2 Study of the Manuscript Troano, pp. 141-161.

366-1 As the term "ideograph" is somewhat broad and comprehensive, it may be well enough to state that I use it as expressing that stage of symbolic writing where the picture characters have so changed that all resemblance to the objects they were originally intended to represent is lost, and therefore they can only be considered as mnemonic signs.

367-1 Study of the Manuscript Troano, by Cyrus Thomas, pp. 142, 143.

370-1 Study of the Manuscript Troano, p. 147.

370-2 Landa's Relacion, pp. 382, 383, Note 1.

www.ingramcontent.com/pod-product-compliance
Ingram Content Group UK Ltd.
Pitfield, Milton Keynes, MK11 3LW, UK
UKHW041658270325
456749UK00010B/414